RIDING THE PASSIONATE EDGE

RIDING *the* PASSIONATE EDGE

Converting Tension into Emotional Intimacy

MARY *and* TOM CUSHMAN

Bennetts Cove Books

Casco Bay, Maine

ISBN-13: 978-0-692-63124-9
LCCN: 2014900513

Cover painting, "Tango Dancers," by Diane Millsap
Cover Design by Alan Pranke
Typeset by Sophie Chi

Printed in the United States of America

For
Chris, Zack, Darby, and Emily

Burn with me!
The only music is time,
The only dance is love.

Stanley Kunitz

CONTENTS

INTRODUCTION

This book was born in a brief, hot encounter between two people who love each other very much. A couple of years ago, after sharply contending for about fifteen minutes with a layered and tricky issue, we finally wrestled it to the ground and, tangled up in laughter and a strong kiss, said to each other: let's write a book, mainly for couples, about living an emotionally passionate life, while avoiding emotional train wrecks.

Unfortunately, emotional train wrecks are all too common. Many of us find it very difficult to skillfully struggle together through powerful feelings, particularly when conflict is in the air, so we often don't struggle at all. Instead, we dodge. We fudge. We pretend. Hoping to avoid a collision, we end up at opposite ends of the emotional couch wanting to reach through the space between us yet not knowing quite how. Listen to a conversation between a man and a woman in a relationship-counseling context, and the picture comes into focus:

Jack and Abby have been married for about nine years. She is vibrant and attractive, younger looking than her forty-three years; he is forty-five, tall, and powerfully built. He gives off a faint air of apology in the way he speaks and holds his body.

Abby: "Jack, most of the time I think I love you, but it also seems as though you push me away. You just never talk about your feelings, or at least not until I pull them out of you, and even then you don't say much."

Jack: "But you're so critical about everything. Most of the time I'd rather *do* something with you—go for a walk or to a movie—than talk, because it just feels as though you're going to be unhappy with me, no matter what I say."

Abby: "Lots of times I *am* unhappy. You talk in circles, and never say what you really mean."

A silence settles between them.

Counselor: "Jack, would you like to respond?"

Jack: "Well, talking to her doesn't feel comfortable. She seems so cold and unresponsive. I have to struggle these days to get her anywhere near the bedroom."

Abby: "See what I mean? You won't even talk to *me*— you talk to him, *about* me! I'm not very turned on by you these days for a bunch of reasons, but do you ever ask me why?"

Jack: "Okay . . . why?"

Abby: "For starters, I don't feel emotionally connected to you, and that makes me pretty disinterested in sex. The fact is, I'm *lonely*, Jack, and I don't think you have a clue what that's about."

Jack: "Maybe not. But I can tell you I'm damned lonely myself."

A collision would seem imminent here. But with two kids, a house they both love, and a future they had hoped to share, it's a collision Abby and Jack would desperately like to avert. The question is, how?

The answer is not by taming their passions and retreating into polite restraint. If they do that, they may die of boredom rather than in a train wreck. Instead, they have to learn how to dig down under their smarting exterior selves, and mine the rich veins of emotional gold that run there. They need, in other words, to go to new emotional depths with one another, and set loose the life they will discover in those depths.

Of course, this is easier said than done. When we detect the presence of fear, anger, grief, or sometimes even joy in ourselves or someone else, we can get unnerved and subtly attempt to shift the course of an encounter. This is especially true with our experience of anger. Anger's explosive power has been clear to most of us from the time we were very young, often making us flat-out frightened of it. Moreover, since anger and love don't seem to belong in the same sentence, we're hard-pressed to believe that the two are closely related. Return to Jack, though, in a conversation with the counselor, a few months down the road:

"I'm amazed," he says. "I now realize that I used to constantly appease Abby to keep her from getting annoyed with me. It didn't work, and we often ended up in a fight. Now that I say what I feel, even when she's annoyed, things are much better between us. It's livelier, and connected in a new way. She says she feels taken seriously and finds me more attractive. It turns out that speaking the truth is sexy—a big and welcome surprise to me."

Living an emotionally passionate life isn't principally a matter of improving our communication skills. Instead, it involves insisting on a certain level of intensity in ourselves and in the relationships we value most—putting who we are and what we need smack in the middle of the table. And doing that again and then again. It means continually moving to the heart of the matter and staying there when—*especially* when—the ground starts to rock, and we want to run.

Most of us have a powerful craving to know another—and to be known—in our closest relationships. Such knowing, however, can't happen unless genuine trust exists. And trust doesn't occur without revelations of truth, which often don't turn out well. Attempts to speak the truth get stalled for multiple reasons: we fear we won't really be heard; we don't know how to say what we feel; we're afraid we'll cause hurt if we *do* say what we feel; we resist making ourselves vulnerable; we fear making a partner angry. So we pull back, inevitably reaping a measure of loneliness.

This book intends to cut through that loneliness. Whether the reader is in a mostly happy partnership, a mostly unhappy one, or somewhere in between, any relationship will at some point get caught in a fog of loneliness. It's the predictable consequence of evading whatever needs to be spoken about. In every instance, though, it's the engagement, the dance, the brave attempt to reach out and build trust *in spite of a lump in the throat* that will drive the fog of loneliness back out to sea. This book is about undertaking that brave attempt. It's aimed at strengthening trust between partners where it's weak, developing it if it's missing, and then exploring how to live into it with gusto. In a word, it's about reaching for a larger life.

The Art of the Spat

In the chapters that follow, we've had to find a word for describing how to deal with emotions that are at least tinged with anger, while allowing for people's anxiety about anger. We've chosen to use the word "spat" instead of fight or argument, because it's a far less threatening concept, and it's easier to respond to it. Despite being a somewhat old-fashioned word, we employ it throughout the book in a deliberate attempt to increase a reader's willingness to see conflict and tension as having a highly positive side.

By "spat," we mean an encounter that's normal, everyday, somewhat heated. A spat will generate fire—but far less fire than a fight. A spat doesn't involve anger bordering on rage, for example, or hurt so severe that a person can do little else but sob or smash crockery, such as might happen if a marital affair has just been revealed. While full-fledged fights may occur only occasionally in an intimate relationship, spats will be commonplace where passion is the currency of exchange. Why? Because we are alive; we can get stung to the quick in an instant; we experience powerful feelings. For emotional intimacy to flourish, we need to be able to navigate those feelings with skill and strength.

Spats are frequently about incidents that may appear small but aren't: bruised desires, dashed hopes, feelings dismissed as trivial, sorrows that can't find a hearing. All these are the stuff of spats—or should be. What's most common, however, is the spat-that-ought-to-have-been-and-never-was. Many spats simply get buried, as does the intimacy that would have sprung to life had the spats been voiced. Spats ride the line between anger and the feelings of hurt or fear that always underlie anger, bringing those feelings forward before they morph into frustrated fury. Spats, then, can be understood as defining the life-giving passionate edge that exists in each of our lives. When we reveal our underlying feelings, emotional intimacy can bloom; when we ignore those feelings, emotional intimacy begins to decline—and sexual intimacy often follows suit:

A husband and wife are attending a large party. In the midst of a roaring good time, it slowly dawns on her that he's been having a particularly animated conversation with a woman they've both known for years. She's not sure what she's seeing, but she's vaguely uncomfortable. On the car ride home, she keeps quiet about her earlier agitation.

Once home, one of two things is likely to happen. He indicates an interest in sex but, still faintly disturbed, she declines without explanation. Or sex does happen, but the woman is distracted. Her unspoken feelings keep her awake later, as the incident grows larger in her mind.

Plenty of people might say that occurrences of this sort are too petty to pursue . . . life is too short . . . maybe he wasn't really flirting. Maybe not, but it isn't the point. Experiences like this one shine a high beam on our avoidance of conflict.

We will often claim that engaging an instance of tension just isn't worth the bother. Life itself, however, has an unpleasant way of flinging that claim back in our faces when the energy in a relationship starts to disappear or goes sour. The truth is that this woman may well have felt a certain sadness, irritation, and loneliness (however subtle) at the party, and she most likely also felt some threat, whether justified or not. If she can summon the courage to risk a spat by skillfully voicing her feelings, not only is the emotional intimacy with her husband likely to go up, but the potential for a full-blown fight is likely to go down. In a relationship that is truly emotionally intimate, there is no such thing as "too small." If someone has a feeling that persists, small isn't the issue. Talking about the persistent feeling, getting heard, and getting beyond it, is.

Spiritual Notes

Learning to have a spat that's productive and that deals with tension creatively isn't just about finding the right words or tinkering with the way we talk. More effective speaking about our feelings will help, but it won't necessarily deliver depth in a relationship. And depth is the prize, the antidote to our loneliness.

At its core, depth is a spiritual matter. And that's why this book—without being overtly religious—incorporates a spiritual perspective, in the widest sense of the word spiritual. In discussing empathy, forgiveness, or listening, for instance, as those factors play out in a spat, we sound a variety of spiritual notes, even as we avoid sounding them too loudly. American culture currently contains a large spiritual paradox: many people are repelled by anything that resembles "organized religion," yet there's also acknowledged widespread hunger for a spirituality that's real, and gritty, and speaks to our actual experience.

That's the spirituality to be found here, in spats as we're defining them. Since all spats contain a live wire, an edge, the potential for creating new emotional and spiritual depth is always present in them—depth in us as individuals and in our relationships. When the tension in a spat is directly engaged and fully resolved, a path is opened to a deeper, more passionate life. And in the end, relationships capable of swimming through deep emotional waters are those that embody the strongest sense of spiritual aliveness.

In order to wrap our arms around the good stuff, however, we have to look first at various ways we sabotage depth. Although these methods of sabotage may seem unattractive, they are cut from the pages of real life and are familiar to all of us. Recognizing ourselves in the initial chapters of this book will clear the ground for the gold to be found further down the road.

PART ONE

HOW WE SABOTAGE EMOTIONAL PASSION IN OUR INTIMATE RELATIONSHIPS

"The brook would lose its song if we removed the rocks."

Wallace Stegner

CHAPTER 1

Avoiding Conflict

An Excess of Reserve

Before exploring in detail why many of us resist engaging in spats, we need to make a claim that we believe is central to that resistance: in our intimate relationships, we are generally too tame, too polite, too reserved, too well behaved. We're not suggesting that people should cut the controls and start indiscriminately yelling at each other. But when a certain level of plain, direct speaking disappears, our intimate relationships suffer. Badly. Consider the following illustrations:

> A husband and wife are at a small dinner party. He says something faintly off-color about women, and she shoots him an unmistakable dark glance. When they are alone, later on, she doesn't revisit this moment of tension. Neither does he.

A woman arrives home from a business trip, crazed with exhaustion, and discovers that her husband hasn't cleaned up the kitchen—again. She is exasperated, and hides it.

The interactions between these couples are reserved to the point of constipation, and in this, they are all too normal. They reveal our general lack of skill in articulating our feelings. They also demonstrate our loss of a certain kind of nerve—a loss that makes sense. It is one predictable outcome of decades spent driving toward "negotiation" between antagonisms and the high marks the culture awards to an attitude of compromise. Obviously, many disputes need to be resolved through negotiation and compromise, particularly in public life. But when these same attitudes get woven through intimate relationships, the transformative voltage needed to keep a passionate connection alive can vanish.

Similarly, political correctness is a highly reasonable constraint when applied to long-standing social grievances. If it seeps into our private interactions, however, that same constraint tends to blunt our emotional edges, and dampen our fire. Though our tiptoeing around conflict is understandable, such avoidance eventually becomes an instrument of sabotage, producing a web of timidities and resentments that ends up feeling like an emotional straightjacket, as the following illustration demonstrates:

Liz and Joe, both somewhat reluctantly, entered counseling about three months ago. Today, Liz is restless and can't seem to focus.

Counselor: "Listen, what's awry here is that the two of you still don't know how to talk straight. What do you think will happen, Liz, if you tell Joe how you feel?"

Liz: "He'll get mad at me."

Counselor: "So what if he gets mad? If he's mad, then you need to hear what it's about so you can start doing something more interesting than avoiding each other's anger."

Liz: "I'd like to believe that, but I don't really trust that he wants to hear how I feel. I'm also scared that if he does get mad at me, I won't be able to contain my own anger."

This example reveals why we tend to deflect necessary spats: fear, hurt, anxiety about expressing anger, and worry that we can't get a full hearing from our partner. These various factors are intertwined within each of us. In order to start untangling them, we begin with what is likely to be the most common anxiety for us all: fear of conflict.

Redefining Tension

Once upon a time, the word "tension" was not automatically heard as negative. It simply meant to stretch, to hold opposing forces in balance. Today, though, in common talk, tension is usually a synonym for emotional stress, and it strikes lots of us as something to evade or medicate—definitely not something to embrace.

But what about seeing tension as an opportunity, as positive? Picture yourself sailing in a stiff breeze. Yes, the boat could capsize, but as long as the rail is up, you are flying *with* the tension, glorying in it. Think of a long-planned surprise party. Once the huddled crowd jumps out with an exuberant "Surprise!" any prior tension was well worth it. Or picture an Olympic slalom skier, straining at the mountaintop gate. Heart-pounding tension fuels the moment, and the skier can't imagine plunging down the slope without it.

Each of these moments generates a certain kind of anxiety, a fervent desire that things not collapse. Each holds a tension most of us would delight in, clap for, and maybe even experience tears over. When events go right, we relish the tension; we call it excitement. We live happily, in other words, with the anxiety that accompanies tension. But when events turn sour, tension turns negative. The sailboat dumps us in the ocean, the surprise party flops, the Olympian hits a patch of ice and crashes—suddenly, *the positive and necessary role tension has played gets forgotten.*

A similar forgetting happens when we round an emotional corner and meet a potential spat. Tension is going to rise, automatically, and along with it, our anxiety.

The skier, as he leaps from the gate, feels in his bones how necessary his anxious tension is. Without it, his run down the mountain will be flat and dull. So he works the tension, rides it, pushes it to rocket him across the finish line. That same skier is almost sure to forget, however, that in his emotionally intimate relationships, tension is equally necessary and beneficial. He forgets that the invigorating presence of a certain kind of tension will spell the difference between a vibrant relationship and a boring one.

Actually, we don't just forget how important tension is in creating intimacy; we don't believe it. Most of us think that emotional intimacy is about the *absence* of tension; that intimacy occurs in dreamy settings with dimmed lights and flickering candles. We are convinced that when tension creeps in, intimacy evaporates. What accounts for this conviction? It springs from our fear of tension's power to ruin things or to worsen a situation with an intimate partner. We don't trust that, if rightly understood, tension will be an ally, just as it is for the skier on his way down the mountain. We don't realize that our attempts to eliminate tension can sabotage the potential for emotional intimacy.

How This Works

Enlarge the example from the start of this chapter about the couple at the dinner party, in their avoidance of potential conflict. When real tension rears its head, the couple tends to do what many of us do: they duck. They don't refer to the incident, yet be sure of this: it's not about amnesia. Neither of them has forgotten the tension-creating exchange. The dirty look she threw at him back at the dinner table found its mark and stuck, like an arrow in a bull's-eye.

From his perspective, it's safer to ignore the arrow, make no reference to it, and just pretend she didn't mean to shoot it. And from her point of view? If she mentions the incident, she risks tapping into an old vein of agitation. She has challenged him before about attitudes she sees as faintly denigrating to women.

Much better to let the party-dust cling. If she even hints at her annoyance, she fears he will sigh heavily, maybe say she's nuts, or ask why can't she leave this anti-woman thing alone anyway.

Those are some of the tricky layers under a spat in the offing. It's complicated, yes, but not at all impenetrable. And letting tension play its rightful role is one key to addressing the complexity.

Here is a sketch of what might happen if one half of this couple decides to go for it and puts the offending member up on the table for discussion. Since the woman shot the arrow, let's imagine that when they pull into their driveway, she's the one to revisit the moment. She doesn't do it skillfully; he, in turn, gets defensive. Tension increases. A few sparks fly. She senses tears pricking the backs of her eyes, and wonders why she didn't just leave this alone, as she'd intended.

But then something pivotal occurs. The woman starts to cry, in spite of her best intentions. The man wants to get impatient with her tears but resists. After some silence, he finally asks her why she's crying. While reluctant at first to admit it, she takes the risk to cough it up and says she was embarrassed at the party, felt slighted as a woman, and her feelings were hurt.

He's quiet for a minute, working through some remaining impatience. More silence follows. Finally, he's able to say he didn't mean to hurt her feelings. He puts his arm around her and pulls her toward him. He says it's hard to admit, even to himself, how much his ex-wife hurt him. He acknowledges that maybe he still harbors some resentment toward her, and maybe it comes out in weird moments, like in misplaced jokes about women.

And so on. All of this is about the couple using tension creatively—riding it, letting it carry them over the finish line. In a later chapter, we will examine much more fully how to do that; how to get to the bottom of a spat and be done with it. For now, we only want to offer the following observation:

If this couple buries the incident, they might well climb into bed that night and make love, but the unspoken note of discord will still lie between them, echoing its faint murmur of alienation. If they have the spat, however, and truly finish it, the strengthened emotional intimacy between them will lead to lovemaking that's sweeter by far.

"Not to take one's own suffering seriously, to make light of it or even laugh at it, is considered good manners in our culture."

Alice Miller

CHAPTER 2

Minimizing the Impact of Hurt and Fear

When Tension Goes Over the Top

While emotional tension contains plenty of positive aspects to enhance our intimate relationships, there are also other sides to tension that need to be given their due. And it is a hefty due, indeed.

When tension between intimate partners rises, keeps on rising, and then rises too high, tension will morph into fear, usually long before we may be aware that fear is even in the mix. And fear can manifest itself at varying decibels. If the volume is low, our fear may translate into a snide comment or prompt our judgmental side to surface. Turn it up a notch and we might be seized by the desire to blame; to locate fault only in our partner, finding not a trace of it in ourselves. Turn the fear up still further, and it can flip without warning into a verbal attack.

If fear becomes full-blown, we may want to strike, or flee, or press our partner into a very small corner—anything to shut him or her off, or out, or up. We might slam a door, run to another room, suddenly entertain ax murder as reasonable, or go as cold and silent as granite. No matter how fleeting these dark thoughts are, if we are squeezed by fear's tightest grip, our feelings and actions are likely to be primitive and extreme. Moreover, when primitive responses well up in us, fear can momentarily freeze us—like a deer caught in headlights. We will probably become reactive and rigid at this point, bent on winning at all costs.

Why do we descend into these embarrassing fifth-grade behaviors? Because each of us, despite our hard-won adulthood, is standing in a well-composted layer of childlike vulnerability. And that mix contains a host of squirmy anxieties that, as adults, we rarely acknowledge: fear of abandonment, fear of rejection, fear of being devalued, even fear that our partner's love could evaporate.

Never mind whether those fears and vulnerabilities are literally true; they can pack a powerful emotional wallop and knock us temporarily off balance in the space of seconds. If we have been wounded by our partner, feel emotionally "cast out," and believe we can't get a hearing, the combustible fusion of fear and vulnerability may push us to be first to grab the abandonment lever. Most of us, after all, in our least attractive moments, want to be sure we hurl the other guy off the ship in the split second before he hurls us.

We all live to rue these fearful and fiery experiences, and we eagerly repress them after the convulsion has passed. But if our fears remain unacknowledged, they control us, individually and as partners. And that's the point. It's crucial to admit our fear, name it, and begin to understand how it works in us, in order to gain any chance at self-control. Emotional freedom actually begins with that self-knowledge. Many of us fail to understand this dynamic, hoping our fears will disappear as fast as they bloomed. They won't. They simply go dormant, like all perennials, and can be counted on to bloom again.

If all this seems like the province of desperately unhappy couples, we offer ourselves as contrary evidence. We have been truly contented for the past thirty years, and we can also fly off the rails of contentment into that compost of old fears impressively fast. It doesn't happen often. When it does, however, if we were plate-tossing types, we'd have a layer of busted dishes littering the floor. That's because there's a daunting paradox at work in this business of our fears and vulnerabilities. *The more deeply we love our partner, and the more secure we believe ourselves to be, the more shaken we can get, in a wounding moment, by the perceived withdrawal of love.* Not real withdrawal, but perceived.

Accounting For Hurt

To understand this paradox more fully, add a layer of hurt (another frequently unacknowledged feeling) to the mix of fear and vulnerability. Most of us can get our feelings hurt easily. It may be difficult for us to pinpoint exactly what we're experiencing, but as a relationship deepens, our vulnerability to being hurt increases. We enter a relationship, after all, because we feel cared about . . . so where is that caring when we need it? The following everyday scenario should make the picture clear:

> A husband comes home in the evening. His wife has been waiting to tell him something she's excited about, but he doesn't seem inclined to listen to her. She's deflated, disappointed. She stumbles around internally, trying to figure out how to talk about her disappointment without provoking a fight. No words work; nothing quite expresses the slosh of resentments and contradictions in her stomach.

Obviously, this is a spat in the making. But the wife can do a lot to prevent the situation from turning destructive by asking herself two questions:

- Am I feeling hurt?
- Am I feeling scared?

In most situations of budding anger, the answer to one or both of these questions is probably yes. If being hurt and scared sounds like bad news, though, here's the good news in the middle of the bad: when we can name for ourselves—and then for our partner—why our feelings are hurt or what we are scared of, we will almost certainly begin to defuse things. Identifying and untangling our feelings may well initiate a spat. Yet, in the process of admitting we are hurt or scared, we create the possibility of expanding the emotional intimacy in the relationship.

Articulating Pain

Why does it work this way? It doesn't always. But talking about what we are feeling at least gets us down to the heart of the issues. Being hurt, or scared, or both is really about being in a kind of pain. And unless we can consciously acknowledge that pain, it will get a grip on the reins and drive us straight into an uncreative fight. Pain penetrates us fast and deep because whatever wounds we experience in the present are invisibly connected to memories of past wounds.

Articulating our pain is the most direct highway to emotional intimacy with our partner. The "disappointment" of the woman, in the example above, is a fancy word for her hurt-bordering-on-anger. She's hurt that her husband has no time, no ears, and seemingly no energy for her. She's also hesitant to speak up, however, because she knows her husband is tired and pointing out a shortcoming may spark an eruption. Therefore, the slosh in her stomach.

This painful brew of emotional hurt and fear can be unsettling and potentially volatile. It's one thing to slice a finger badly with a kitchen knife—it hurts like crazy and may send us into a momentary panic, but everything can be bandaged up reasonably fast. Emotional pain, however, cuts far deeper. Imagine a profoundly painful exchange, such as a wife unexpectedly telling her husband she can't stand the sight of him anymore and that she wants a divorce. Whether or not the divorce actually happens, healing such an outburst may take a very long time.

But even much milder moments of discord—such as a sense that my partner devalues my opinion—can also pierce to the emotional quick. That quick is like an old-fashioned canvas tent in a downpour: touch the tent on the inside and a drop of water will form, ready to fall. It's the same when our interior "canvas" is touched. Whether we're aware of it or not, our tears sit at the surface and can spring out with minimal pressure.

This Is Too Much Work!

Now, right here, we come to a juncture where a number of readers may want to throw up their hands and flee. Who wants to live so emotionally close to the bone? No wonder we want to sabotage effort like this . . . it takes too much time, too much focus, and energy we don't have! What happened to the concept of just accepting differences? No one can possibly address every slight from a casual dinner conversation or dry every tear. Don't we simply need to buck up and let certain things go?

Our answer is yes . . . and no. Yes, there is a lot in our partner that we must accept. Even contented relationships have to tolerate moments of emotional distance. No two people resolve every difference or settle every score. All of us, as adults, live with our share of hurt and fear, some traces of which will never be fully erased.

It's the "no" part of the equation, however, that prompted us to write this book, because one conclusion stands out above all others: the road to real and lasting emotional passion lies directly through the thicket of our thorniest feelings. And it's a great irony that it actually takes far less time and energy to deal with these thorny feelings than to bury them.

If it's true that we are secretly controlled by whatever we have buried inside us, then that truth has multiple implications in any spat. This is especially the case with buried pain. No partner, after all, is a mind reader. If I haven't told him how heartbroken I am about not having children, how is he supposed to know why I might come home depressed from a baby shower? And what will happen when I'm irritated by his lack of sensitivity? A conversation that's likely to go south in a hurry.

Here's the unpleasant fact: unless we become skilled at tapping into whatever pain we're feeling and talking frankly about it, someone other than our best self is going to keep showing up in our relationships. And emotional passion will eventually wither. Conversely, when we are able to trust a partner with that pain, exposing our vulnerabilities, emotional passion can blossom.

Sure, it takes time. And energy. And effort. The learning curve is steep and can be initially discouraging. We may want to blurt out in exasperation, why didn't anyone teach me this? Where was I supposed to get the skill to handle all these complicated feelings? We understand the impatient desire to declare a halt, yelling, "I'm happy enough! My partner and I have a great time together! Why do I want to *bother* with all this?"

Our answer to that very good question is, you want to bother because happiness and joy are two different things, and the treasure worth diving for is joy. Happiness is mostly a one-dimensional phenomenon that can be fitted nicely onto a Hallmark card; joy can't. Resisting domestication, joy is more likely to be found running free, braided thickly together with fear, tension, high and holy laughter, sorrow, and a host of other spirited, life-affirming feelings.

The experience of giving birth to a child perhaps describes most closely what we mean by joy. The far flatter word, "happiness," isn't much of a match for the wildly complex and contradictory emotions involved in the birth process. Take the feeling of anger, for instance—seemingly an unlikely bedfellow for a child making its way into the world. But women and men alike report feeling flashes of intense anger as part of the tumbling, joyful river that raged through them at their child's birth. It makes sense. Because births of all sorts are that complicated—and that good—including the birth of passionate emotional intimacy.

"Our cosmic fights, when I think the end of the world is come, are so many broken shells around our growth."

Sylvia Plath

CHAPTER 3

Running from Anger

Anger Is Inevitable

Another way we sabotage passion in our lives is through our handling of anger. While hurt and fear are complex, anger carries even heavier freight. Of all our emotions, most of us identify anger as causing the greatest trouble, so it's no wonder that lots of us want to flee from it as fast as possible.

Since anger is often misunderstood, we need to define what it is up front. Essentially, anger is the primal, adrenaline-driven emotion that kicks in when we're hurt or scared, to the point of believing we must protect ourselves. Anger is mostly a defensive emotion, but it can quickly shift and become a vehicle of attack. Think of a shield: we may hold it up in defense but if necessary, we will use it as a weapon.

Anger is inevitable—if we have a pulse and are alive to a full range of feelings. Consider the hurt and fear we experience if we're unjustly accused. When that happens, we often feel swift, intense permission to vent our anger, to correct the sense of injustice.

Anger constitutes a court of last resort. When events make us sufficiently fearful (emotionally or physically), our anger will often overtake us and burst past the boundaries of composure we normally maintain. The following example shows how anger is, at bottom, a means of self-preservation:

> All her life, a middle-aged woman and her mother have been in a contentious relationship. The mother has always been critical and an angry perfectionist; the daughter has a lifelong feeling of not being good enough; of never being able to get things right. After fearing her mother's angry rejection and impossible demands for so many years, the daughter is finally overcome by the need to fight for her own soul. Pushing through her fear and hurt, her anger spontaneously takes over, and she confronts her mother with her long-buried rage.

It's easy, perhaps, to identify with this daughter. But the mother may only be repeating behavior she experienced as a child from her *own* parents. Ideas about anger tend to be deep and durable, in part because, for many children, anger is often followed by punishment, and that punishment may even have turned violent on occasion. There's nothing odd about wanting anger to get the hell off our emotional premises—now.

Attitudes toward Anger

Our attitudes toward anger usually have a shelf life as long as our memories. Think of the various "messages" about expressing anger that we received from our original families, such as *anger solves nothing; nice girls don't get mad; just stow it right now, little buddy; if you can't say anything pleasant, don't say anything at all; when you get over it, you can come out of your room.* The messages are clear: it's best to avoid anger—or bury it completely.

Additional attitudes about anger can also be shaped by other authority figures in our lives. If we trust an adult and then experience a skewing of that trust through spasms of bad temper or even abusive behavior, we will be quick learners: anger and danger are spelled almost alike.

Understandably, many of us reach adulthood with a well-honed aversion to anger. This aversion explains, in part, why it's the rare person who can get angry effectively, without cutting a swath of destruction, and then return relatively fast to a place of equilibrium and forgiveness. Anger usually combines undercurrents of hurt, fear, and vulnerability into one unstable concoction. When that concoction blows, and the feelings boil over, it's hard to maintain our grip on a controlled level of anger.

Restraining Our Fear of Anger

Rare or not, though, the person with a skillful grasp on anger does reveal a crucial ingredient for a successful spat: the ability to tether fear of anger. Anger itself is not the chief problem; our *fear* of anger is. The ghosts of past experiences haunt us, and we fear that our scary history with anger will repeat itself. Which it might. For example, unless the daughter in the previous illustration learns how to deal with anger in a new way, she's likely to end up resembling her mother more than she might wish. The ghost of her mother's anger will continue to skulk around during future spats, scaring the daughter and agitating her emotional waters.

Restraining our fear of anger is a tall order. Recall a moment when anger stalked the perimeter of your consciousness. Did this happen without accompanying signs of fear, such as your pulse quickening or your stomach tightening? Probably not. Fear tends to follow anger like a shadow, and separating the two emotions is difficult. But that separation is what needs to occur when we have a spat: experiencing anger in the present, while keeping our ancient fears of anger at bay. The fear that chaperones our anger can't be completely eliminated any more than a shadow can. But once we understand our fear's particular "shape," as it conforms to us and to our own history, it can usually be corralled, and prevented from overwhelming us.

As an illustration of this process, return one more time to the couple in the car after the dinner party and to the woman pressing forward with the spat. When she revisits her husband's comment about women, she will surely feel her anger surfacing anew and right alongside the anger, some old fears. She's afraid, because of past history, that her husband will see her as foolish and overly sensitive, and he'll get mad at her.

She almost ditches the impulse to initiate a discussion. After all, she could get mad herself if he misunderstands her. She decides to wade in, and although it may be somewhat unconscious on her part, she "keeps her fear at bay" by trusting that this might be a new moment. Despite her fear, she shares her hurt feelings and allows herself to cry. Her tears blur her fear. Now, speaking from a more truthful place, her anger starts to soften.

The man, meanwhile, keeps his own fear in check when he sets aside his initial impatience over her tears—impatience being low-level anger, grounded in fear. As a result, he is able to "hear" her tears and be penetrated by them. Between the two of them, this couple restrains their fears enough to create a larger emotional space. Now able to listen to each other, they move slowly beyond their fear and hurt toward a resolution.

No matter the source of our own fear of anger, the outcome for most of us is similar. Exactly because of that fear, when we do experience anger we often don't express it directly. We're not skilled at modulating it; we rarely clean it out completely. As a result, we can end up with a closet full of "anger costumes," ranging widely in color and style—from excessive politeness, to mean talk, to terminal cheerfulness, to sarcastic one-liners, to an anxious inability to stand up for ourselves—each costume trimmed with fear.

Misshapen Anger

Although our anger may not come out straight, it will come out eventually. And like lightning, it has to go somewhere. But where? It's important to answer this question because "bent" anger, in any form, greatly complicates the process of having a spat. In fact, some misshapen expressions of anger actually prevent meaningful and intimacy-producing spats from occurring. The first and most obvious illustration lies in the phenomenon of bickering.

Bickering may look like the-spat-that-won't-quit, but it isn't. Instead, it's an endless series of partial engagements that never get off the ground. The same issues arise over and over, caricaturing intimacy, never finding resolution. The anger between a pair of bickering partners may appear to have life, but the life is best understood as stillborn, because the trademark of these engagements is that they don't bear fruit, just more bickering. There's plenty of anger here, often a great excess of it. In a particularly perverse irony, however, this kind of anger short-circuits the relief that comes from effective spats. Bickering operates like acid: if allowed to drip constantly onto a relationship, it will fully corrode anger's cleansing power to generate emotional passion.

A second illustration of anger that does not come out straight is familiar to many of us: talking with great fervor to . . . the showerhead. Or the dashboard, or the dishwasher. Whatever the target, it's never the real one, and it's guaranteed not to be able to answer back. That's why we're talking to it; for whatever reason, the true object of our anger is too scary to approach. Though this behavior is self-defeating (we expel the energy of our anger without settling anything), it does have one saving grace. If we're listening to ourselves, we might hear what ought to be spoken in person. In other words, the private mutter-fest we're having points directly to the actual spat that needs to occur.

There are a variety of other forms of indirect, or incomplete, anger, such as snippiness, irritability, and being quick to get annoyed. These behaviors happen when we don't allow ourselves to feel anger fully enough by discharging it accurately and effectively. Take note, however: when someone is snippy toward you, he or she probably is mad (hurt, fearful) about something, but it may have nothing to do with you. A spat could be indicated, but it's smart not to jump into it too fast.

In American culture these days, we are quick to take offense; we seem to have our emotional guns constantly cocked. Outrage rides the range like a refugee from an old-fashioned western, overeager for a showdown . . . if only at the office water cooler. It would be wiser by far to keep our guns holstered and focus instead on cocking our ears, since real listening almost always precedes someone's decision to disarm.

"To love and be inattentive is a contradiction."

Marv Hiles

CHAPTER 4

Imagining We're Listening . . . When We're Not

Many of us pride ourselves on being good listeners and will protest any suggestion otherwise. There's a certain shame in being dubbed a "poor listener," and we're embarrassed when told we talk too much. Listening . . . talking . . . too much . . . too little—not surprisingly, all of this can add up to a flashpoint in the matter of spats. In any spat, particularly between intimate partners, feeling listened to looms large. Consider this familiar exchange:

> She: "You're not listening."
> He: "I *am* listening!"
> She: "You're not."
> He: "I hear you!"

Behind any faint echo of rueful humor in these words, it's also easy to detect strains of anxiety, defensiveness, and perhaps most loudly, competitiveness over who's right. It's impossible to overstate how ruinous our attempts to be right are; the drive to be right destroys intimacy. It also kindles a subtle and mostly unacknowledged loneliness.

When we need someone's listening ear and fail to get it, we can mark the spot: that's where loneliness begins. Loneliness might seem too strong a word, but poor listening and loneliness are tightly woven together. If we don't feel listened to, we're going to feel isolated and alone. When partners, even happy ones, get frustrated in their desire to be heard, loneliness builds, and a spat will gather on the horizon. If that spat is sidestepped, layers of hurt will thicken and further lower the potential for any real listening to take place.

Blocks to Listening

In order to change this dynamic, we first have to grasp the factors that block our capacity to listen to each other. Some factors are external: the busyness that afflicts everyone in modern life, our endless multitasking, the dizzying speed at which many of us live. All of these devilish forces contribute to a profound "unquiet" that impedes our ability to listen.

The internal blocks to listening, however, are much more significant than the external ones, and they play a far greater role in sabotaging our chances for emotional intimacy.

Self-absorption is one such block. We may be so focused on ourselves that we barely hear another's need for us to listen to them. We might say, "Right, right," when someone speaks to us, but his or her desire to be heard doesn't penetrate our hearts enough to open up our ears.

Despite a surface attention, self-absorption usually means being focused elsewhere. A person caught up in a self-absorbed moment, for example, will sometimes speak more loudly or even "talk over" your words while you are still speaking. Instead of your words and feelings being taken in and responded to, they bounce back to you. They may be superficially acknowledged but are unregistered and therefore not heard, not received.

This reminds us of the story of the man who visits with a Zen master, in hopes of learning about Zen. While the master quietly prepares tea, the man talks continuously about his view of Zen, his ideas, his thoughts, his questions. As he speaks, the master pours the man's cup to the brim with tea—and keeps on pouring. The man finally yells, "It's full! No more will go in!" The master replies, "Like this cup, you are full of yourself. How can I show you Zen?"

Lack of "presence" is another block to listening. The "un-present" person is not so much absorbed in himself as he is _unaware_ of a deeper reality—his own, and yours too. The "sealed-offness" of a person texting on a cell phone while in the company of others is an obvious example of being un-present.

But think also of someone who stares out the window during a conversation, or continues to watch the television screen while a partner is talking. Presence implies receptivity and focus on what's happening right here, right now, with the other human beings _in_ our presence. It means being able to hear our own feelings and hear someone else's as well. An un-present person, unable to hear himself, is also unlikely to hear anyone else.

Anxiety, in multiple guises, is frequently the most significant reason our ears shut down. Recall how anxious we can get when we're criticized, judged, or misunderstood. If any of these accusations or their close relatives show up, we are likely to start closing the doors on our ears, if only because we've begun justifying ourselves.

Fear of silence, rooted in anxiety, creates an additional barrier to listening. If we perceive silence as an anxiety-charged vacuum, we will likely want to fill it with noise—fast. For some people, silence can be more stressful than a roomful of screaming children, and the need to break the silence can become overpowering.

When any block to listening occurs, we tend to move into conversations that trade mostly in superficialities, which will, in turn, lead to a faint but pervasive sense of hollow loneliness and a feeling that emotional receptivity is in short supply. For example:

> A wife says, "I sometimes get the sense that my husband doesn't really want me to talk about my feelings. He usually deflects me when I try."

> A husband says, "Between her job, the kids, and the house, my wife is so absorbed I can't find her."

> A college student says about her widower father, "When I'm with him, I feel lectured; he tells me what I ought to

be doing. I just wish I could talk with him about some things that are bothering me, like missing my mother."

A woman says, "My friend seems so focused on herself; she almost never asks me about my life."

All this amounts to a "deafness" that neither speaker nor listener may realize is occurring. It's a disconnection, often driven by both people, that can remain completely unidentified. It begins with deafness in relation to our own feelings, extends to deafness about other people's feelings, and leads eventually into "deaf responses" to one another. For instance:

A man tells a friend, "My father is dying." The friend responds, "How old is he?"

A husband admits to his wife, "I'm anxious about my new job." The wife says, "You'll do fine."

A woman says, "My friend Jane doesn't call me anymore." Her partner replies, "She's not much of a friend."

Intimate Listening

Responses like these may come from the mouths of well-meaning, loving people, yet they reveal considerable deafness. All of them *track away* from the feelings of the original speaker. On the surface, they pass as conversation, but they are not a road to intimate conversation—which is what someone focused on the death of a parent, or anxiety about a job, or the loss of a friend is likely to want. If real listening means being emotionally present, striking into intimate ground, and making a satisfying connection, then these responses don't pass muster. Whatever the source of the "deafness"—anxiety, distraction, defensiveness, or some other kind of warding off—the result is the same: speaker and listener are not joined at the level of their feelings.

In a long-ago anecdote about love and loss, the dancer Isadora Duncan talked about how difficult it was to get anyone to listen deeply enough to her feelings following the accidental drowning of her two young children in a river. People encountering her were themselves so distraught over the accident that they would either persist in changing the subject or talk about the children's deaths in ways that completely missed the emotional reality of Duncan's distress. She simply couldn't get others to understand that what she needed above all else was to talk about her children, to remember them—not as an intellectual exercise but as an emotional and spiritual one: to "re-member" them and thereby pull their bodies and souls close to her again.

Bereft, despairing, and stricken with loneliness, Duncan reported that it wasn't until she visited a woman who flung open the door to her house and embraced her, exhorting her to "tell me all about the children . . . I want to know every single thing you can possibly tell me about who they were," that Duncan felt she could finally collapse into her overwhelming grief.

This example, while taxing, captures the loneliness to which we are referring. But people experiencing far less dramatic kinds of deafness, or isolation, can also feel terribly lonely. If our feelings don't get a full hearing, or our emotions fail to register with another person, loneliness then begins its work, filling in the spaces. When that happens, we experience the peculiar feeling that others don't "get" us—and not being gotten is a seminal source of loneliness.

Deaf Responses

It isn't always easy to recognize when we have fallen into a deaf response. Since many of us remain plagued by deafness, however, either in a partner or in ourselves, we're going to bear down with further illustrations to expose the problem more fully. Does it seem as though we're flogging the subject? We aren't. Emotional deafness is so pervasive and troubling that its importance can't be exaggerated.

The following three categories start with the most glaring examples of deafness and move in descending order to more subtle ones. All the illustrations, however, display an arrow pointing in the same direction: away from real listening.

1. *Missing by a Mile*

- One friend says, "So tell me about your job." The other friend replies, "Things are really pretty tough." The first friend says, "I know . . . let me tell you what's happening at *my* job."

- A woman says to her husband, "Your sister called last night." He replies, "I'm really concerned about her." She says, "Everybody has problems."

- A woman admits, "I'm nervous about this doctor's appointment." Her boyfriend replies, "Don't worry; he's supposed to be a good guy."

In these examples, one speaker makes a direct bid for listening and help, and the other person misses it. This borders on a willful kind of deafness because although the plea is pretty clear, the listener doesn't register it.

2. Overlooking the Clue

- She says, "Wow, I can't believe I'm turning fifty." He replies, "You're not old."
- She asks, "Did you sleep okay last night?" He murmurs, "Sort of." She says, "That's good."
- She says, "I'd love to have my brother over for dinner sometime." He replies, "What time are the Smiths coming on Friday, anyway?"

The need to be heard is less obviously stated here. Nevertheless, it's as though one person drops a clue like a handkerchief on the sidewalk, and the other person walks right past it.

3. Curiosity Eludes Us

- A husband says, "You're looking kind of down in the mouth." His wife doesn't respond but nods a vague assent. He says nothing further.
- Upon bumping into a friend, a woman says, "Hi, how are you?" Her friend replies, with a dubious tone, "Okay . . ." The first woman launches into talking about herself—at length.
- A wife says: "I've just had an interesting meeting at Sarah's school." Her husband says, "Yeah, I wondered when you were coming home."

While there's nothing so overtly "wrong" with these responses, they do demonstrate how common it is for us to display only a minimal level of curiosity toward what others say. Our tendency is not to follow up, not to pursue. Will the woman in the second illustration ever actually ask what "okay" means to her friend? Unless a person clearly trumpets an "Oh, my God, I'm in trouble," message, many of us are likely to snap back into our own preoccupations. It's as though we already know everything we want to know about someone before we encounter him or her.

In an emotionally passionate life, there's an attitude of "radical curiosity." This is different from an appetite for information. It's a hunger to know and connect with another human being at a level other than the superficial. We don't mean to imply intrusiveness; where no curiosity is invited, it would be entirely unwelcome.

But when curiosity is genuine, it's experienced as an invitation. It feels like an opening, a willingness *on the part of the listener,* to form a deeper connection. Radical curiosity is an entirely other order of listening, devoid of the prurience of gossip and the casualness of chat. It's an essential ingredient in the seedbed of qualities we need to develop if we want to stop sabotaging emotional intimacy.

PART TWO

HOW WE CAN STOP SABOTAGING INTIMACY IN THE FACE OF TENSION

Listen, or your tongue will keep you deaf.

Native North American Proverb

CHAPTER 5

Develop a Spirit of Deep Listening

Necessary Capacities

To engage in a spat that will go anywhere other than straight down involves at least the following three elements: affection, will, and skill—all of which amount to cultivating a particular spirit or set of the heart. Affection may have been momentarily suspended because one or both people are seeing red, but for a spat to succeed, both partners must still believe they are cared about. Each also needs to possess a certain will—a drive toward common ground, shared hope for a resolution that isn't about "winning," and a genuine desire to heal rather than hurt, even though a well-placed jab might feel just fine at the moment, thank you.

The skills needed for a good spat are many-layered, just like the troubles that take us into a spat in the first place. Those skills are all learnable and get much sharper over time, and when our affections and wills are lined up, the skills assume their rightful place. For now, however, we want to focus on some capacities of the spirit—like real listening, and empathizing. We'll then go on to explore the skills that bring those capacities to life. Let's put it this way: when we need to say something difficult, or painful, or embarrassing, our skill with particular words and phrasing won't matter as much as the spirit behind the words.

We're aware that the terrain here is mountainous and rocky, especially in regard to the subject of feelings. Much dark ink has been spilled in recent years over the idea of "getting in touch with our feelings," to the point that the expression "touchy-feely" now borders on a slur, evidenced by the curled lip that usually accompanies saying these words. Actually, the phrase touchy-feely deserves to get buried, because it's silly and doesn't bear any relation to the complex realm feelings inhabit. Rocky or not, we're going to scale these mountains because it's impossible to have a worthwhile spat without knowing how we feel. And we don't mean knowing as a mere mental exercise, but knowing as a gut experience.

To whatever extent we lack capacities for listening and deep feeling, there's a strong likelihood that energetic emotional engagement in our lives will proportionally diminish. Whether in relationships between partners, close friends, or family members, the same equation is at work: keeping emotional intimacy alive requires voltage. Sustaining that voltage is a complex matter implied throughout this book. For now, it's the building blocks, the capacities, that need addressing, beginning with the one underlying all the rest—the capacity for listening with a lot more than just our ears.

Developing a Hearing Spirit

If all of us, in certain moments, can be guilty of deaf responses, as defined in the last chapter, then all of us have a stake in understanding what makes those responses so profoundly unsatisfying, as well as a stake in fixing them. By "fixing" we don't mean adjusting a phrase or an attitude so that we'll appear more attentive. The conversion of deaf responses into hearing ones isn't a matter of buffing up a few surfaces but rather of reaching for a seismic shift in the way we approach listening in the first place.

We are used to thinking about the task of listening as just that: a task. And one that we perform with our ears—with any luck, as quickly as possible. Listening understood this way carries, like all tasks, a faint whiff of duty, foot dragging, and a do-I-have-to. It feels like something imposed rather than chosen; a burden we're glad to shoulder off when the task is done.

What happens, though, if we pour some heart and soul and a willing spirit into the ears we bring to our listening? Before long, if we persevere in the effort, with energy and affectionate regard for ourselves and others, we may discover that we have swapped duty for pleasure, and burden for delight. Converting deaf responses to hearing ones is, in the long run, a spiritual pursuit. It's about becoming a certain kind of person rather than a more skilled technician. Anyone, after all, can learn to parrot the psychological jargon, "I hear you saying . . ." But it takes a deeper wit and wisdom to listen with the "ears of our hearts" to another human being and really absorb, into the very marrow of our bones, what they are telling us. When we can do that, *we ourselves become the richness and the realness* we are seeking from someone else.

Real listening is not about altruism or being a good scout; it's about getting a larger, richer life for ourselves and, secondarily, for those we love. It's principally, though, about developing our own being, our own spirit, to the point that others experience us as a resonant sounding board with ever fewer degrees of deafness.

Listening as an Art

Listening, as we are intending it here, involves bending ourselves fully toward something or someone else and temporarily surrendering our self-preoccupation. Since real listening is more art than science, more capacity than technique, it may be made plainer by looking at how various artists do their work. Consider:

- Any actor aspiring to give a credible or moving performance must start by listening completely into the character he is trying to portray.
- A poet must become a listener to life in all its guises; when listening stops, so does poetry.
- A concert pianist, hoping to stir the souls in her audience, has to first listen into the intent of the composer and then fully open her own spirit to the music she's playing.

Understood this way, it's clear that real listening is about becoming a person with specific strengths that involve all sorts of capacities beyond mere technical skill. Listening does take skill—and plenty of it. But skill alone won't get us where we need to go—in poetry, or piano playing, or intimate relationships. The essential requirement is the cultivation of certain qualities of being.

For example, think of visiting an ill person in the hospital. We're tempted to come up with cheery comments, distractions, or funny stories, when actually the only necessity is just to *be* there. Whatever follows next requires openness to mystery; no fancy footwork or verbal acrobatics are called for. To many ill people, the prospect of having visitors is exhausting for just this reason: visitors think they need to entertain.

Now imagine a hospital visit with a dearly loved, dying spouse. It's instantly obvious that what's needed is to leave anxious talk at the door, and bring one's *self* to the bedside. One's listening, fully-in-the-moment self, excruciating though the moment may be. It doesn't have much to do with finding the right words. Instead, it's about being present, about "standing in" with someone, about listening to whatever that someone has to say without counting (or not yet counting) the cost to oneself.

The exact same capacity to "stand in," to be present, is what's required in a creative spat with an intimate partner. It might seem like a stretch to compare the agitation of a partner locked in a spasm of anger to the needs of a dying spouse, but in terms of the listening being sought, they're not far apart. The same qualities of spirit in the listener are needed in both cases.

A Specific Illustration

Jeanne comes roaring into her husband, Bill's, office, fit to be tied about something she's sure he's done. She has on a massive head of steam and is convinced not only of her own absolute rightness but of Bill's complete and utter idiocy as well. She can't remember at the moment why she married him.

Bill's first reaction to her, when she barks out her initial words, is to say, as he closes the door and sits down, "I don't understand. . . I really want to hear why you're so angry."

Bill's initial response begins to reveal the spirit of a listening person. In order for him to even make such a response in the first place, though, he has to have a host of capacities to bring to the encounter. These capacities may seem hidden and subtle, but they are indispensable to a creative spat.

1. Bill could be overwhelmed by the volume of Jeanne's anger when she blows through the door, but he isn't. He doesn't panic. He also doesn't react to her anger with some version of his own.

Many things are going on here that illuminate Bill's ability to listen. He's quiet at first and waits. This keeps him from fanning the flames of Jeanne's anger. At least for the moment, he adopts an attitude of suspended judgment and a preliminary willingness to forgive.

Despite being mostly silent, Bill remains engaged. His sitting down invites conversation, and his few words speak a willingness to get his ears on. Keeping a rein on his own anxiety, he escapes being swallowed by the storm Jeanne is caught in. She may have dropped into a "fifth-grade moment," as described earlier, but Bill doesn't join her there. His posture of "waiting" sets the stage for a productive spat, despite Jeanne's anger.

2. He doesn't immediately decide he's to blame, just because she says he is.

Bill doesn't adopt Jeanne's frame of reference. He doesn't give her the power to be judge and jury of the situation, and he doesn't automatically agree with her conclusions about whatever has gone wrong between them. She could prove to be right; he may have done something he will come to regret. But he isn't intimidated; he stays grounded in himself. He also isn't defensive. He's clearly prepared to listen but won't let Jeanne define the terms of the spat. He'll take responsibility for himself and only assume "blame" where he thinks it's accurate.

3. He focuses on her feelings.

Despite the widespread temptation to leap foursquare into "the facts of the case" and start a debate over who did what to whom, Bill resists. The pivot-point of the conversation is Jeanne's feelings; those feelings **are** the facts of that moment.

Bill is patient when the initial focus needs to be on Jeanne's strong emotions—not on information about what he did or didn't do. Until she experiences her anger being heard, Jeanne won't be able to hear anything else. Whatever Bill is feeling has to get set aside for a minute.

4. Without patronizing her, Bill waits for Jeanne's anger to run its course. It's likely to do so fairly quickly because

he doesn't bolt, emotionally. Instead, he receives her anger directly.

Bill makes a critical move: he takes Jeanne seriously. Despite being very angry, she is not abusive. And his ability to absorb her fury into himself begins to diminish her anger's force. This doesn't happen through long speeches but by Bill's capacity to stay present to the intensity of Jeanne's feelings and forgive her for being caught in the moment. Moreover, because of his calmness, he's likely to win back a piece of respect from this woman who, mere minutes before, couldn't remember why she married him.

The Role of Empathy

Bill and Jeanne's spat (which we will return to in a later chapter) doesn't just profile a listener; it profiles an empathetic listener. Bill demonstrates a willingness to walk in the shoes that are tightly pinching Jeanne's feet, as well as a detached capacity to "hear into" her anger. He hears *beneath* her anger and into the pain she's obviously experiencing.

Empathy is a particular kind of listening that takes a little doing to fully grasp. It sounds simple but isn't. This much is clear: without empathy, a creative spat is virtually impossible; with empathy, we have an excellent chance to find one another—and stay found.

One way to understand empathy is to contrast it with its cousin, sympathy. Though empathy and sympathy are often used interchangeably, they are not the same. Sympathy is an emotion that runs largely along the surfaces of our lives. We can say to someone, for instance, that she "has all our sympathy" and mean it. When we say it, however, we don't necessarily feel any emotion. We might have some feeling, but if we really think about it, we can see that we've often expressed sympathy without experiencing a deep reverberation of emotion inside ourselves.

And that's fine. Sympathy is mostly a means of communicating compassion. The collective wheel wouldn't turn very well without it, because the kindness and concern that accompany sympathy are aspects of caring for each other and being members of the human community. At the same time, expressions of sympathy almost always involve a certain distance, a measure of remove from whatever pain is experienced by the person to whom we're expressing our sympathy. In a nutshell, sympathy can exist with no real emotional cost to ourselves.

Not so with empathy, which always comes with a personal price. In empathizing with another human being, we give a piece of ourselves so that the person may begin to be shoehorned out of an experience of pain. Think back to the illustration about Isadora Duncan and the friend who was willing to hear about—and absorb—Duncan's pain over the loss of her children. The root of the word empathy, originally from the Greek, means "to feel into." It involves setting aside one's own needs in order to enter another person's emotional world. And that doesn't happen without a cost.

Or look at Bill, just described. He surely had his own feelings when Jeanne burst into his office. But he put those feelings on hold momentarily, so that he could "feel into" Jeanne's anger in a full way. It's not that Bill's own feelings don't matter; of course they do. But what matters more, initially, are

45

the emotions that underlie and drive Jeanne's anger. No one gets as mad as she did without suffering from other, more primary feelings. And Bill understands this. He's able to perceive the hot river of hurt and fear coursing under the mask of her anger, and he sets his own feelings aside in order to hear into hers. In some zone far inside himself, he can hear himself *in her*, can identify *her* feelings as sometimes also existing in him. That's empathy.

Much deeper, much more immediate than sympathy, empathy is, at bottom, a "listening into" suffering. It may seem surprising or strange to cast Jeanne's anger as a form of suffering. But if a partner is truly angry, he or she is suffering from anger, and the caring response is compassionate empathy. It's no accident that the word "compassion" means "to suffer with," and the word "patience" shares the same linguistic origin. What Bill communicates to Jeanne when he sits down and invites her to tell him what's wrong is exactly this: patient willingness to incorporate her suffering into his own self. Conversely, an *im*patient response communicates an *un*willingness to suffer with another person. The truth is, we can't listen into someone else's suffering without touching into our own. Therefore, it costs us. Sympathy is a milder, less expensive version of compassion; empathy is the costly first cousin.

Here's another way to understand the cost of empathetic listening. Recall how difficult it can be to sit with a person who is in tears. If tears—even racking sobs—are given time, they will eventually subside. But crying can be scary, especially when someone's tears feel as though they may spill out of control. We're afraid that if we offer comfort, we'll just increase the very tears we're wishing would stop. Part of us wants to get impatient, run away, do anything but remain present and "listen into." And yet the irony is that patient listening to tears is what will enable the person to stop more quickly. It doesn't happen, though, without a distinct emotional cost to the listener, who has to tamp down his or her own anxiety firmly enough so that the crying person can believe real solace is at hand.

We're aware there's room here for confusion. People sometimes think of empathy as simply stating, perhaps with great feeling, "I hear you," or "I understand you." While there's nothing wrong with these sympathetic expressions, empathy asks much more of us.

A person in need of empathy, such as Jeanne, first has to get her emotion (anger, in this case) listened into, as described above. That leads to a sense of being cared for. But someone in Jeanne's spot doesn't trust she's been heard until the hearing is paired with a believable and trustworthy response. At this point, Bill might have descended into defensiveness, but he doesn't do that. Instead, he sits down, and earnestly asks Jeanne to tell him more. This may seem like a small move; its simplicity is deceptive. Sincerely entering into it requires a major shift of the heart . . . another way of understanding the concept of "cost."

Here's an example of that shift in action. We all know how irritating it can be when we're hoping for an apology from someone (actually, what we're hoping for is an empathetic ear), and instead we get a weary sigh, followed by, "I've already apologized ten times." That remark is a direct tip-off that no apology has yet registered with the person needing to hear it. And ten more won't make any difference. It's not the "I'm sorry" that matters; it's the set of the heart uttering the words.

People yearning for an apology know whether their partners have an empathetic tilt toward them. And the tilt doesn't even have to involve words, although when an actual apology is truly in order, the words better be there. But empathy can also be conveyed by a knowing look, or a tender gesture, or even attentive silence. Whether spoken or wordless, however, genuine empathy usually demands quieting down, slowing down. Perhaps most important, it also demands a curb on our tendency to problem-solve, to "fix." That's what the ten-time apologizer is really doing—trying to fix the problem into going away; trying to still evade whatever trouble caused the need for the apology in the first place. Trying, in other words, to evade the cost.

The Alchemy in Empathy

Empathy, in short, is one of the price tags on a passionate life. And the returns we receive in offering it far exceed its cost to us. The reason is simple. There is alchemy at work in the process of empathetic listening: *both* parties in the exchange undergo a certain transformation, and so does their relationship.

In the example of Bill and Jeanne, it may appear that Jeanne receives the greater benefit. But the pile of emotional gold reaped by Bill is perhaps the larger of the two. It contains at least the following: the dignity of being constructively helpful to a loved partner; a reduction in loneliness or alienation; expanded understanding of himself and Jeanne through the encounter; an increase in closeness; and a rise in self-respect.

Without empathy, the spats we need to have will either not occur or be destructive, and the emotional passion between us will ultimately fade. With empathy, passion has a chance to blaze like a field of Dutch tulips in the springtime. Cultivating empathy, therefore, is all about feeding the very fires that keep love alive—not a bad return for a pair of listening ears.

The Place of Humility and Forgiveness

Almost without exception, an empathetic and compassionate person will also possess a certain humility. But humility is a quality easily misunderstood. While having humility does imply a definite absence of arrogance, it's more revealing to trace its roots to "*humus*," which is best translated as earthy. People with a right-minded dose of humility are not likely to have a lofty opinion of themselves but rather to be unpretentious and down-to-earth.

For the person trying to listen empathetically, humility is crucial because it's the prerequisite for another necessary element in the listener's spirit: forgiveness. Forgiveness depends on humility and is nourished by it.

We are not referring here to popular notions of humility, which are excessively self-deprecating—a clear sign of false humility. Genuine humility demands acknowledgement of our flaws, a strong stripe of self-acceptance, and an absence of perfectionism. All these, in turn, spawn a spirit that is both self-forgiving and forgiving of others. The emotional result compares to the layered nature of earthy humus—humility down below, forgiveness above it, and empathy on top.

The word forgiveness, like humility, can sometimes sound in our ears with a faint ring of weakness. We intend it differently here. We don't mean forgiving in the passive sense, such as letting something go, not making a fuss, or overlooking what shouldn't be overlooked. Such forgiveness frequently arrives cloaked in sentimentality and is correctly perceived as lacking in grit.

In the truly forgiving person, there is no absence of grit; forgiveness fully conceived is one of the most strenuous emotional and spiritual disciplines. While it has its soft, yielding qualities, forgiveness requires backbone and strength under pressure.

Consider the behavior of the Pennsylvania Amish community in 2006, when a rampaging gunman entered a schoolhouse and mowed down ten girls, leaving five of them dead, before he committed suicide. Rather than being filled with vengeance, the Amish response (which included the dead children's parents) was stunning in its sweep. Not only did they contact and extend forgiveness to the gunman's family, but they sat with his wife and children at his funeral.

While this illustration of forgiveness is startling, the forgiveness asked of us in the course of our normal lives can also demand plenty of starch in the emotional collar. Think about what happens when we are hurt, and likely angered, by someone we love. For sure, it will take courage for that person to seek forgiveness from us, but it will take just as much strength, perhaps more, for us to do the forgiving. Offenses sting, and make us burn with resentment. The all-too-human part of us wants to burrow down, prop up our pride, and righteously tend the flames of indignation, which plays, of course, right into the hands of smallness of spirit.

The Source of Forgiveness

It's the larger and wider part of us, however, that's evoked when forgiveness becomes an issue. In the example of Bill and Jeanne launching into a spat, it may not immediately seem as though forgiveness is part of the mix, but it definitely is. One can see it in Bill's willingness to allow for less-than-perfect behavior in Jeanne. This willingness has to be based, in part, on his knowing something about his own imperfections, his own capacity to go off the deep end. It has to be based, in other words, in his own humility. And that is, indeed, the heart of it. Forgiving someone else has everything to do with the humbling awareness that we ourselves sometimes need—and long for—forgiveness.

If we can accept that Bill (on his best days) does seem to demonstrate ample humility and forgiveness, then the question is, what is the source of those qualities in him? With the Amish, it is starkly clear: they are devoutly religious people with a deep commitment to the active forgiveness historically urged by all world religions, even in the face of terrible events. One might say forgiveness is in the Amish bloodstream. But what about someone who might not necessarily call himself religious— perhaps someone like Bill—for whom religion may be mostly a blank or even a point of hostility?

Regardless of one's religious grounding—or lack of it—for all of us there is a kind of spiritual economy at work. We can only give away what we possess, and we can only forgive with the degree of forgiveness we've already integrated into ourselves. The Amish were not deluded. They were thrust into the ground of their particular faith, and the ground held. Although Bill's encounter with Jeanne is obviously of another order, it's nevertheless true that to respond the way he did, Bill had to be listening to an interior voice more loving and more just than simply his own momentary self-interest.

Forgiveness isn't spun out of airy hopes. In the long run, it's a discipline, a strength, that comes from honoring a voice we all carry within us. That voice emanates out of our larger, deeper selves, rather than out of our smaller, fearful selves. Some people call this deeper voice "God"; others name it our True Self or our Best Self. Regardless of the name, what matters most is the behavior and the spirit that the voice encourages us to adopt.

When Bill let Jeanne's angry outburst stand for a moment, and didn't react in kind, he was listening to this voice and took what is sometimes referred to as a "holy pause." Such a pause may be seen as the equivalent of a deep breath, but it's also a conscious attempt to let the water of our best selves rise up from the well within us. If that water carries a strong measure of mercy, is non-judgmental, contains no trace of the heavy metal of perfectionism, and is filtered through forgiveness, then it's "holy" by any meaningful definition of the word. In this regard, it's worth pondering that the words holy, health, and whole all share one linguistic source. Bill's holy pause, in other words, is a strong nod in the direction of health and wholeness in his relationship with Jeanne.

Anyone hoping to enjoy strong, passionate relationships—with friends, family, lovers, spouses—has to find the humility to see himself clearly and let himself be seen by those to whom he wants to be close. This means living not just with some abstract allowance for "the flawed nature of humankind" but with a keen appreciation of one's *own* flaws. To expect a relationship that's long on affirmation but short on challenge about those flaws is to yearn after a kind of permanent immaturity.

The simple truth is that we have to forgive ourselves and one another for our indelible humanity and find the belly laugh at the bottom of our own interior well. That laugh reverberates with feelings of all sorts. Accordingly, we now tackle the large subject of making sense of feelings—and developing the skills needed to hear the feelings of others.

"[H]is mother died, and the summer was lost to grief and boredom and numbing inarticulate silences at home with his father. They had never discussed feelings and had no language for them now."

Ian McEwan

CHAPTER 6

Embrace New Listening Skills

Feelings Are Primary

The first skill a listener requires is a full understanding of feelings—and the need to engage them with gusto.

We're accustomed to thinking of feelings as wispy and ephemeral . . . in some sense, no more substantial than a passing thought, not meriting our attention. At least not usually. Of course, most of us would agree that an experience of real sadness, or fear, or anger, or joy is plenty substantial and should certainly be given lots of emotional room. An odd mist of impatience, however, can surround the entire subject of feelings. And especially in regard to so-called minor matters, there's a faint conviction that many feelings ought to be passed over relatively fast, without undue fuss.

This minimizing approach to feelings doesn't help much in reaching for a passionate life or when there's a spat on the horizon. To put a fine point on it, feelings *are* the "facts" in a spat and are the engine for every spat that ever unfolded, anywhere, for any reason. A spat without feelings is a contradiction in terms, because without feelings, no spat would occur in the first place.

It isn't that every single feeling has to be addressed; the prospect is absurd and exhausting. But in regard to relationships, our feelings are primary. If we seek passionate intimacy, we need to listen not only for deeply rooted feelings but also for feelings we may be prone to disregard. We will often set feelings aside, whispering things to ourselves like, "Oh, that's so petty I can't bring it up." And we imagine that's the end of it. But lots of spats go underground at exactly this juncture, only to muster down the road as a battalion of resentments that have rearmed in the dark.

The peculiar dilemma we face in regard to the way feelings work in a relationship is that all of them carry significance, and not all of them need attention. The job is to figure out which is which.

While some feelings may be only minimally important, our ineptness and impatience in regard to feelings in general means that we can easily fail to hear when a feeling (our own or someone else's) issues from depths that can't be ignored. It's as though feelings register on an invisible "scale of significance," from one to a hundred. Unless a feeling rises to a fifty on this scale, we may not even be conscious of it, and it could take a reading of seventy-five to make us speak up.

We don't delay because we're stupid; we delay because acknowledging feelings can cause discomfort. It's as though we become anxiously "shy" in the presence of feelings, because we don't quite know what to do with them. If they're on the upper end of the scale and force us to speak, we'll probably blurt them out. Further down the scale, however, many of us will seek a path to slip away, hoping to evade a feeling's grasp.

The problem is the vulnerability that's attached to our feelings. Admitting what we feel has a way of stripping us down to our emotional skivvies, exposing what we care about, and raising the specter of being misunderstood or dismissed. It makes sense that we usually move slowly when revealing our feelings, exercising caution over who will get access to them.

This caution, natural as it may be, has to be overcome in an intimate relationship. The skill of bringing feelings to the surface—and staying with them—will largely determine a spat's outcome. We talked earlier about listening to a person's tears and said that patient listening will usually end the crying sooner. Likewise, the ability to be patient with feelings is essential during a spat, because it indicates a willingness to care, in more than a cursory sense, about what someone is feeling. If patience is absent or is on the brink of mutating into impatience, the other person's impulse to express feelings will shrivel. When feelings are surging around in someone, looking for a way out, the other person must be able to respect the existence of those feelings, and listen up.

Feelings are really not wispy or vague at all; instead, they are the core of our nature and have their own definite heft. But there's a huge paradox here: while our feelings are solid and strong, they are also in constant flux. This means that as we change (and we do all the time), our feelings are changing also—an unsettling idea, making it difficult to trust them. Our feelings *are* trustworthy, eminently, but at the same time our wariness makes sense. If feelings are distinct, yet their very nature is to be in flux, discomfort seems like a reasonable response. And that's just where we often fetch up: mistrusting our feelings, being edgy around them.

Mistaking Thoughts for Feelings

This edginess could partly explain why, as "feeling instruments," we are often not finely tuned and why it's so common for us to misidentify thoughts as feelings, as in the next exchange:

Counselor: "How did you feel, Alice, about Jason's comment?"

Alice: "I think it was wrong."

Counselor: "That's a thought, not a feeling. What did you actually feel?"

Alice: "I didn't like it."

Counselor: "We're getting closer. What did you *feel?*"

Alice: "I felt frustrated."

Counselor: "And is frustrated a polite word for angry?"

Alice: (laughs) "Maybe . . . yes . . . I guess I *was* angry. And I still am."

It can be tricky for us to move down from our heads, out of our thoughts, and into experiencing our feelings. Thoughts are less threatening, less anxiety-producing, and create less vulnerability than feelings. Like Alice in the above example, we feel safer with thoughts. Thoughts are abstractions, removed from our emotional center, while feelings are usually right up close. It makes sense, therefore, that we often employ tamer words in the realm of feeling, calling ourselves frustrated, for instance, rather than using the bolder word, angry.

Mixed Feelings

We can also become confused about our feelings when they seem to conflict, such as feeling grief *and* relief after someone with a long illness finally dies. But mixed feelings are a common experience. In any single moment, if we could drop a plumb bob down into the pool of our feelings, we would discover that we are juggling a host of feelings simultaneously. Imagine being at a child's school play and the wave of feelings that might wash over us: fear that our kid will mess up but also pride that she's on the stage at all, aggravation over the scheduled hour of the play, joy, empathy, delight, and so on. Our feelings are not in any sense "pure" or one-dimensional; they are usually jumbled together, making them hard to sort out.

Similarly, we can't control whatever feelings arise, as much as we wish otherwise. And that can be disorienting. We might be able to maneuver our thoughts, but our feelings will usually outmaneuver us . . . at the precise instant we hoped they wouldn't. For anyone who has ever spoken at a funeral, this has perhaps become distressingly clear. We gamely swallow our anxious feelings, but they keep threatening to rise back up again and choke us. Or how about walking a daughter down the aisle to be married, or attending the college graduation of a seventy-year-old parent, or anticipating a much-loved soldier's return home at last—after serving in a war—now severely wounded. All such moments will generate a flood of feelings, and we can't control that flood any more than we can stop a moving river with our hands.

Of course, we do continually make choices about acting on our feelings. And since feelings do come largely unbidden, we need the skill to guide their direction and outcome. Initially, we must ask ourselves whether a feeling warrants any action at all. It might just be a superficial sensation or a momentary flash, and perhaps we can simply watch it come and go. We will often discover that a feeling merits only self-reflection, rather than being brought up to another person.

Take the example of feeling irritated. Maybe our irritation is tied to something troubling in an intimate relationship and therefore needs to be voiced; or maybe we are nursing a minor irritation out of proportion because we like the adrenaline it delivers. In any instance, much can be learned by looking at ourselves first and then deciding whether a feeling needs to be articulated. There's trickiness here, though, because such deliberating plays right into our avoidance of conflict. One easy way to determine whether to speak about a feeling is to track its persistence. If it just won't quit and seems to come from some deep place, then we need to talk about it. But as much as possible, we want to be reflective and responsive, rather than unreflective and reactive. That comes from being as clear as we can about what we're feeling.

All this adds up to a pretty challenging picture; small wonder the concept of "getting in touch with our feelings" earns such jaundiced press. Yet this area of experience is one we can ill afford to treat lightly. Feelings are the language that connects us to our own emotional life and to the emotional lives of others, whether in a spat or not. Without our feelings, we would have no doorway to intuition, wisdom, or any sensitive knowledge of human nature.

In the previous section on lack of emotional presence, we said that becoming present to others is all about first accessing what *we* are feeling. If we are unaware of our own emotional depths and flat to our feelings, our responses to others will mirror that same flatness. For emotional intimacy to exist, feelings have to kindle an answering echo between people. When that echo exists, if someone says, "I'm sad," or "I'm irritated," we know what he or she means because we too have experienced sadness and irritation and can therefore summon a resonant reply.

A Vocabulary of Feelings

In order to truly become a listening person, we need to develop a nuanced "vocabulary" of our feelings, which will increase the strength and effectiveness of those echoing responses. Creating such a vocabulary can be done with any feeling, but looking at how anger works demonstrates the point most swiftly.

Moving upward from milder forms of anger to Code Red, an "anger vocabulary" would include at least the following words: bored, troubled, upset, miffed, bugged, annoyed, peeved, resentful, agitated, aggravated, offended, sore, exasperated, indignant, pissed off, infuriated, enraged . . . out the door! While all of these words express anger, they definitely describe different levels of experience. And the nuances among the words turn out to matter a lot. Once we feel the difference between "annoyed" and "infuriated," we can see why we need the skill to vary our responses accordingly.

In the absence of an anger vocabulary that helps us consciously name our feelings from mild to strong, it's very difficult to gauge the depth of our anger soon enough, when we're just starting to get mad. And low-level anger for which we have no accurate words is likely to unconsciously build until it explodes. The following experience reflects the spiral in which many of us can get caught:

"When I'm mad, I often don't realize it. At least I usually don't say anything for a long time. I can feel my blood pressure rising, I just don't express it. I'm surprised by how fast I can get pissed off. By the time I actually speak up, I'm often furious. I say awful things and then I don't know how to get out of it. I can scare my wife—and my kids—when this happens. I end up feeling crappy about myself."

If we lack a nuanced vocabulary, and we can't name our feelings, we still continue to feel them. And our behavior may then quickly fly out of our conscious control. We might go silent, we might noisily slat around, but as we begin to mount the emotional ladder, with anger compounding itself at every rung, there's precious little that can happen except for us to blow. An anger vocabulary keeps us straight about what we are feeling and when—far, far down the ladder. It gives us the opportunity to check ourselves before we launch into the stratosphere.

In a spat, this kind of early warning system can make all the difference. When we're aware up front what we're feeling and can articulate that awareness, we head off unconstructive conflict before it has a chance to seize control of the situation. Simultaneously, we get far more access to the emotional layers in one another, strengthening the emotional bond between us.

"Oversensitive?"

We offer here a strenuous counter to a lament frequently heard in relationships: that one person is "too sensitive." There is no such thing. Sensitivity isn't the problem. Accusing someone of oversensitivity is simply a shortcut to shutting that person down, trying to win the point. The issue is *managing* sensitivity, not eliminating it, and managing it well can be complicated.

For example, if we are overcome by hurt whenever a partner tries to be candid with us, we are not managing very well. We can't use our sensitivity as an excuse for ignoring something we need to hear about ourselves. At the same time, the person labeling someone else as "too sensitive" needs to ask and answer this: Am I creating enough emotional "safety" for the supposedly oversensitive person to really get heard? If not, it's a sure bet that the one labeled " too sensitive" will clam up. No one can rightly be called thin-skinned in the face of criticism, if the criticism is delivered harshly, clumsily, or with disregard for whatever pain may be inflicted. Clams, after all, are well practiced at hiding under the sand.

Keeping Our Ears Open

While handling feelings is a central part of listening, the single overarching skill needed to become a first-class listener is this: *when we're in a conversation, and it's our turn to listen to someone else, we have to learn to block the impulse to speak.* That sounds easy, but separating listening and speaking is like trying to pry apart a closing elevator door. The overwhelming likelihood is that our tongue and our ears will get fused, ensuring that we won't be skilled as either listeners or speakers.

In any conversation, of course, listening and speaking do alternate continuously—that's a chief reason why it's difficult to put any space between them. Doing so not only takes skill but even more important, it takes rock-solid commitment on the part of the listener. If our commitment to becoming a great listener is at all flimsy, that's exactly what the quality of our listening will be: flimsy and fleeting. When we can take to heart the skills described here, though, listening can truly become life-giving, especially in an intimate relationship. That's particularly so on occasions when a spat is brewing. Spats demand a willingness to keep our ears open and our mouths closed at the right moments, and spats will deliver a high reward when we manage that process with a graceful hand.

Four Concrete Listening Skills
<u>Skill 1: Become keenly aware of how selectively we listen.</u>

For a partner hoping to get heard, the worst damage to that hope comes from what's known as selective listening—meaning selecting what we want to listen to and tuning out the rest. To some extent, we're all constantly selecting. Everything we hear intersects with our philosophy of life, as well as with our attitudes, assumptions, and aggravations. We ourselves, in other words, are always part of the listening/speaking "mix," and it takes real focus to quiet our own nattering interiors enough to be fully available to someone else.

Cozy up to this uncomfortable truth: even with those we may dearly love, selective listening is what many of us do, much of the time. We assume we know what the other person is intending—and especially how he or she is feeling—before we've been told. Or perhaps we've previously heard some version of what's being said, and we resist giving the information headroom yet again. In a variety of situations, selective listening becomes our default, so that whether or not we've actually "heard it all before," the Select button gets pressed through force of habit. And there the damage occurs. Information may get discarded, but the other person's feelings are attached and will follow the information right out the window.

We're particularly prone to listen selectively when we're verging on anger, because anger makes us prickly about what we will let in. Think of the old story about the husband and wife who are in an argument with each other, during which he decamps to the grocery store with her list of ten items. She yells after his departing figure, "Just *don't* forget the eggs!" and of course they're the sole item missing from the bag when he returns. He "selected" out those eggs and mentally broke the whole dozen over her head.

Or think of a couple bickering over some ancient, unresolved issue. It won't be long before one person (probably interrupting the other) blurts out, "I know exactly what you're going to say!" demonstrating the durability of our temptation to mind read. The moment we slide into reading someone else's mind, we have hoisted the Flag of Selective Listening, and its loud flapping will deafen the conversation.

Every subsequent skill involved in real listening is tied to our selectivity. Getting conscious, then, of our habitual inclination to only more or less listen enables us to hear afresh just how much editing—in and out—we do in our conversations.

Skill 2: Get good at listening to *both* facts and feelings.

If there's a single junction where intimate relationships invariably go off the tracks, it's at the whistle-stop where facts and feelings are flying by, mistaken for occupants on the same train. They are not. They ride on separate but converging tracks, and failing to recognize this invites a collision.

The most common error for us, as listeners, is to hear only the facts and at that, our own version of them. We tend to focus on the facts, not taking into account the feelings that always shape those facts. For example, a husband says, "Damn it, we never *agreed* that your parents were coming for Thanksgiving."

It isn't that a pending parental holiday visit doesn't matter— it does—and yet that fact only sits on the surface of a comment like the husband's. What matters much more is the undertone of feelings that can always be heard beneath the facts, if we're listening. Much of the time, however, feelings (the drivers of every spat) simply aren't talked about. We are affected by those feelings, but unless we're consciously naming and discussing them, we act as though they don't exist. And many a collision occurs at exactly this spot. More accurately, this is the moment spats turn into fights. When overly focused on the facts, we forget that no fuel burns as hot as the failure to get one's feelings heard—fully.

The facts-versus-feelings problem gets clearer by extending the previous "who's coming to Thanksgiving dinner" comment beyond the husband's initial—and obvious—aggravation:

Wife: "Well, we did talk about my parents being here for Thanksgiving."

Husband: "But that was weeks ago, and we never came to a clear agreement. I haven't heard anything more about it."

Wife: "I said I thought they would be glad to be invited."

Husband: "Maybe you did. But you know how difficult they are when they're here. I thought we'd have much more of a conversation about it before we decided what to do."

Wife: "You never brought it back up, so I assumed it was okay to invite them."

Who had the facts fully straight here? As usual, neither party. We all remember facts differently because our "facts" are always intertwined with our feelings. It isn't hard to imagine the unvoiced feelings that could have prevented both the husband and the wife from returning to this sticky conversation.

From the husband's point of view, he might have felt relieved that since he'd expressed his annoyance over her parents often enough in the past, when his wife didn't bring the subject up again, it meant she'd been discouraged from inviting them. She, on the other hand, well aware how irritating and disruptive her parents could be, might have felt anxious about revisiting the subject, wanting to avoid rekindling her husband's annoyance, and she simply carried on solo. She was only too happy to assume he'd relented, causing him to drop the subject.

The unacknowledged feelings here are driving the misunderstanding. Unless the couple can go down under the facts and discuss their feelings, including why neither of them brought the issue up again, the spat is likely to become a fight, with each person convinced his or her own version of the facts is correct. Both people's facts need to be heard through the emotional lens of their feelings in order to resolve the disagreement.

Skill 3: Commit to forming your answers
only when it's time to give them.
In any conversation, it's so common for us to formulate our responses while someone else is still talking that we almost don't recognize we're doing it. Yet once articulated as a problem, the

nearly universal reaction is a sheepish grin, a flush of crimson, and the admission, "I do that *constantly*..."

We said at the start that when it's our turn to listen, we need to block the impulse to speak. But the task is even harder than that. We not only have to stop the actual words from leaping off our lips, but we also have to block the *intense internal drive to line those words up*. This is difficult to do, because much of the time our minds run on ahead of the other person's speaking. By definition, though, if we let our minds do that, we're no longer listening; instead, we're getting ready to talk.

This is what happens. Someone speaks and, before long, something that person says captures our attention. Right in that instant of capture, we begin formulating our answer, with listening starting to fade. And the real problem? People almost always delay saying what's most important to them. They usually save it for the end of a sentence or a story. But what if, by then, the other person has long since actually stopped listening? It's plain: the notion that we can simultaneously listen and get ready to speak is an illusion. We have to alternate these two behaviors; otherwise, any real listening will stop at exactly the point where we begin forming our response.

There are some straightforward explanations for what's going on here. First of all, a measure of anxiety is almost always part of the conversational picture—very tempered anxiety, perhaps, and often invisible but present nonetheless. When we're forming our responses, we're frequently anxious that we won't remember what it is we want to say or that our own thoughts will get buried if the other person talks too long. Alternatively, our competitiveness may surface and cause us to worry that we'll lose our conversational "advantage," especially if we're headed for an argument. We don't do any of this deliberately, but because we can zip so quickly into these behaviors, they can feel deliberate to the other person.

> "You never let me finish!"
> "I can't think when I'm talking to you!"
> "That isn't at all what I was going to say!"

Frustrated comments like these are clues from the speaker that the listener hasn't yet mastered the art. It's actually an act of great trust and intimacy to remain quiet and receptive when we're in the listener's shoes . . . hanging in with the other person, being genuinely impacted by what he's trying to tell us in the present moment, getting drawn into *his* depths. It involves believing that we can listen without being swallowed by the other person's reality, surrendering to the moment at hand, and trusting that our own moment to get heard will come.

This process may seem nerve-wracking, but we can give ourselves to it with confidence for one reason: *when we, as a listener, open ourselves to someone else, the odds are that person will begin to be curious in return and will open his or her own heart to us.* And right there—right exactly there—our deepest yearnings start to be satisfied. Because to feel really heard, to feel someone "gets" us at the level of our unspoken loneliness, almost inevitably produces relief, attraction to the other, gratitude, and respect. All these responses, moreover, increase the rich alchemy of emotional intimacy—an outcome that will forever elude us if we succumb to the shallower satisfactions of forming our responses in advance.

Skill 4: Decipher words; be sure their
meaning is the same for each person.

This may sound like the smallest listening skill to grasp, but it can create a large amount of trouble if overlooked. For example:

She says: "I'd love it if we spent more time together."

He says: "Wait a minute, wait a minute . . . we spent lots of time together yesterday."

These two people clearly have different concepts of what it means to "spend" time together. She may mean she wishes they had more time for intimate conversation; he may mean they did many things together yesterday, which took plenty of time. Whatever the specifics, most of us do far too much inferring, and we regularly fail to check out what people actually mean by their words. At the least, words signal very different things to people—just think of someone saying "my father" and the widely divergent associations those words can carry.

If someone says, "I didn't do well in school," it's impossible to know from the words alone what that statement signifies to them. Does it mean they got a B when they thought they should have gotten an A? Were they measuring themselves against fierce pressure and therefore could never in a million years have claimed they "did well"?

When listening, we need to let *others* explain and stay with them until they divulge their own particular meaning. This means listening for the feelings behind the words. Having so rarely received listening of this sort, most of us don't expect it to happen. When we do receive it, all someone else has to do is

71

look into our eyes: the proof that we've been deeply heard will be shining there like a star.

All these skills, in combination with the listening spirit detailed earlier, will result in becoming a perceptive and empathetic listener and will draw us into relationships of ever greater emotional intimacy. But it should now be clear why listening like this levies such a high personal cost. It's hard to wait, to be patient, to set our own needs aside. It takes great forbearance to give silence an upper hand. Every impulse in us wants to press forward, loosen the reins on our impatience, and let our own energies surge out the barn door like a young horse. In other words, all that we want to do, we can't do. And we also can't retreat into veiled disdain, wishing the other person would hurry up and finish talking. Instead, we have to lay down our straining impatience and reach instead for the nourishing gains that real listening delivers.

The Riches of Listening Well

And what are those gains? First, when we set aside our own self-preoccupation, we can drop down into a quieter place inside ourselves and find the pleasure of having nothing to do but attend to someone else. We get freed for a moment from our own hidden but ongoing struggle to be noticed and heard, and we receive in exchange the self-respect that comes from caring for another.

Second, as a direct result of this shift in our attention, we can experience ourselves as being a more giving, more expansive person than we thought we might be—a realization that brings subtle but distinct joy.

Third, there's a further lessening of loneliness and an increased feeling of connectedness, far below the surface. Anxiety decreases, replaced by gratitude for being able to be "right there" with someone else. In the end, roominess of spirit expands the heart, driving out tightness.

None of these gains should seem odd; just think of what happens to us when we are drawn into other experiences of deep spirit. Recall hearing a majestic piece of music or a great poem, or seeing a theatrical performance that lifts the hair on our head. We may not understand it exactly, but in those moments we know ourselves to be experiencing the mystery of our common humanity. We can feel ourselves stunned into silence, yet growing larger in response to what we're hearing. In a sense, another "person" emerges in us in these moments. Call this person our Best Self or our Real Self; call it God-in-us. It's what gets born when empathetic listening happens.

These emotional gains are rendered more obvious through the following experience of Mary's:

"Some time ago, we were standing in an antiques shop in New Hampshire, when I spied a small, well-worn pillow-like object. Its top was embroidered with the words *Welcome, Little Stranger* and a date, 1841. I felt instantly pierced by this pillow, correctly guessing that it had once been a present for a newborn baby. Despite having beloved stepdaughters and now much adored grandchildren, I've never had any biological children of my own, so such moments will sometimes kindle a still-smoldering spark of sadness.

"Actually, a little involuntary sound escaped me when I realized what the pillow was, which drew Tom to see the object himself. Once I explained, he murmured swift understanding of my response, given his long acquaintance with my indelible (if now only occasional) sorrow. He asked if I wanted to buy it. With faint ambivalence, I declined, and we soon went on our way.

"Late that night, in a motel room in Vermont, I woke up and then was unable to go back to sleep. It wasn't long before I realized that a part of me was back in the antiques shop, still struck by the poignancy of the phrase, *Welcome, Little Stranger.* In a few minutes of pondering this, I felt the early waves from the storm of tears that issues from only one source, and I tried to swallow them. It didn't work. And though he'd been sound asleep, Tom was soon curled up behind me, which of course made me cry harder.

"There are many reasons why I love my husband, and know myself loved in return. The exchange that happened next, though, shows not only where that love is grounded but also the hope that's implicit in this book. As we lay there, I eventually, by way of explanation, choked out the words, "Remember that little pillow?" Whereupon, he whispered, "Yes," and drew me in closer.

"Like many emotionally intimate moments on the passionate edge, this one was freighted with patience, intensity, and empathy, which is why, despite the loneliness implicit in the topic at hand, I didn't feel lonely—because I wasn't. In contrast, had his reply been "What pillow?" (not an unreasonable response, so many hours later), prompting a need for me to remind and explain, the moment would have produced a loneliness too complicated to describe.

"As it was, years of slowly coming to understand each other, years of multi-layered discussion around the entire subject of childlessness, along with spats that resolved and integrated heartfelt longings for both of us . . . all this created the empathy in Tom that erased any possible loneliness in me."

Experiences like this are the durable result of the intimate, sustained engaging we're describing. They aren't inevitable; they are sometimes elusive. But when we try faithfully to develop a listening spirit and the matching skills, these experiences will become more and more the measure of our days and eventually outline the passionate edge of our lives. Is it work? Yes. Work that's worth the energy required? Yes, beyond any doubt.

"Out beyond all ideas of wrongdoing and right doing,
there is a field. I'll meet you there."

Rumi

CHAPTER 7

Commit to a Spirit of Conscious Speaking

The capacity to listen effectively is just one half of the equation; speaking effectively is equally as important. When a spat is in the air, we need to be extra conscious of how we speak to someone else—being keenly aware that we can set off a firestorm in a hurry.

Anxiety's Powerful Role

When we speak, nothing assumes greater weight than our own anxiety, and that's complicated when so much of our anxiety may be unconscious. For us to speak in creative and emotionally grounded ways, we have to figure out how to curb our anxiety and stop our anxious talk. If this appears at first glance to be a minor concern, consider the following example:

Rachael and Ted are having a conversation about her impending entry into law school after a fourteen-year hiatus as a stay-at-home mother. She's excited, and she's also as nervous as a cat.

Ted: "What's there to be anxious about? You'll be as smart as anyone else in your classes—smarter than most."

Rachael: "I'm feeling really stupid. I'll be at least a decade older than everyone. Just the thought of *registering* for the classes makes me want to die of anxiety!"

Ted: "Rachael, that's crazy. I've been living with you for a long time, and you're as competent as they come. I'm not going to listen to this dopey worry that you're 'stupid.' It doesn't make any sense."

Rachael: "'Dopey?' Thanks a lot. That's so helpful. I'm trying to tell you I'm scared about not being smart enough to do this, and the only word you can come up with is dopey. Last time I checked, Mr. Brilliant, that meant stupid."

While Rachael's anxiety comes through the loudest in this spat-quickly-turning-into-a-fight, Ted's own anxiety is also a likely factor. One might well ask: what does *he* have to be anxious about—she's the one going back to school. True enough, and yet he may also be anxious, admitted or not, about various things: money that's going to be spent on this venture, how a return to graduate school will alter their family life, what it might mean for them as a couple if Rachael meets a whole new circle of people, whether her interest in law will lessen her interest in him.

Anxiety is a wily adversary, insinuating itself into conversation and consciousness in disguises often difficult to recognize. When we're speaking with someone who is already anxious, it's imperative to become increasingly aware of our own anxieties and quiet them down. Failing to do this will inevitably stoke the anxious fire that's burning in the other person.

Enter Detachment

To manage our own anxiety we need, as speakers, to achieve a certain spirit of detachment—not coolness, not disinterested non-caring, but a detached engagement that creates momentary emotional distance. This is a paradox. In order to be truly emotionally close with someone else, we first need a degree of separation from that person. The reason is simple: to whatever extent we lose our detachment, our separateness, we also lose our ability to bring our most creative self forward, and we tend to lock on to the other person's emotional curve. That's exactly what Ted does, as his own anxiety "fuses" with Rachael's. When she veers into catastrophizing the re-entry into school, Ted follows her anxious lead—and over the falls they go in the same barrel, plunging toward a fight.

Alternatively, if he lets her anxiety penetrate him to the point of evoking his empathy and brackets his own anxiety while holding onto his detachment (again, not chilly, just separate), the chances of confining this encounter to the limited heat of a spat are vastly improved. In addition, Ted and Rachael will surely draw closer to each other if Ted responds more like this:

> *Rachael:* "I'm feeling really stupid. I'm a decade older than everyone. Just the thought of registering for classes makes me want to die of anxiety!"

> *Ted:* "I can hear that it's scary, but I'm not sure I understand why. Maybe we can talk this thing out, and some of the fear will go away."

> *Rachael:* "Thanks . . . talking about it with you might help a lot."

> *Ted:* "It might help me too. I'm now realizing that I'm not going to find your return to school easy, either."

Acknowledging and then taming his own anxious concerns enables Ted to make one of the speaker's crucial emotional moves: shifting from impulsive reactivity to thoughtful response. Unrecognized anxiety spawns our reactivity, and reactivity is the highly flammable fuel for most fights. But when we're detached enough to manage our anxiety, we are less likely to snap into reactivity.

Personal Authority
In order for the spirit of any speaker to be strong, he or she must grasp the connection between detachment and personal authority. Genuine personal authority doesn't turn power over

to someone else. Instead, it trusts its own instincts, its own voice. The words *author* (to give voice to) and *authority* come from the same linguistic root. When we are rightly detached from someone, we can be connected to her yet stand firmly in our own authoritative voice—not stepping into her emotional shoes. The person may get completely wrapped around the axle or even come unglued, but that's about *her*. We don't have to follow suit, as Ted did in the initial example.

In an intimate relationship, both partners need to be clear about their own authority; otherwise, tension will build. For instance, if we overstep the boundaries of our authority by sharing opinions and feelings when no such sharing has been invited, we'll be experienced as intrusive, controlling, and annoying. Alternatively, we may "understep" our authority by expecting a partner to do the emotional work we need to do for ourselves. But if we sit back passively, making our partner dig for our desires and feelings, he or she will eventually be wearied and annoyed by this approach as well.

Imagine the irritation that might seep in when partners have agreed to go to the movies, but then, in picking which movie to see, one partner replies, "You decide, I don't care." Passive responses like this seem benign, but they actually may aggravate because they push the other person into a role he or she didn't request. For a relationship to be in balance, we need the reverse: partners who are clear about their own desires and feelings, in matters big and small. Unfortunately, while such clarity is vitally important, it can often be mislabeled as selfishness.

Right-Minded Selfishness

The idea that there could be anything positive to say about selfishness throws lots of us into a mental tailspin. Despite new approval in the past couple of decades about self-care and tending to one's own emotional well-being, most of us are inclined to recoil if a partner says, "That's so selfish." Just hearing the word "selfish" might drive us to slink off into the scorn we fear we deserve. And sometimes we do deserve it. If "taking care of ourselves" has occurred at someone else's expense or without enough thoughtful consideration, squaring off with our selfish behaviors would be a very good idea.

But right-minded selfishness is different; it's about knowing and revealing our own emotional and spiritual needs. For instance, if we have a need for solitude or spending time with friends, not honoring these needs will fan anger at ourselves and breed resentment toward our partner. Wishing others would mind-read our needs is just another way of inappropriately asking them to take care of us. We have to grant *ourselves* authority to take care of ourselves. Of course, if we are silent about our needs, we can avoid all accusations of selfishness. But we will also end up muddled about our own real feelings and desires, and we will find our personal authority sharply reduced.

Whatever form right-minded selfishness takes for us, it involves continuing to ask and answer the following two questions:

- What do I most deeply want?
- What do I most deeply feel?

Initially, such questions might sound selfish. But if we're seeking a relationship of passionate emotional intimacy, they are vital and provide the soil for real intimacy to thrive. Without knowing what we truly want and feel, we can't develop a speaker's spirit that is wise and authentic.

In addition, our ability to answer these two questions is a measure of our own personal authority. We get help with the answers from plenty of others, but we will only be satisfied when we can finally answer the questions for ourselves. And anyone we accept as a partner must be able to do the same.

Effective Speaking

When all these pieces are in place—better-managed anxiety, sufficient detachment, and a stronger sense of personal authority—we can begin to communicate much more effectively. Note the differences in the following responses during an infuriating conversation:

> "I just want to explode and walk out when you talk
> to me like that."
>
> vs.
>
> "I feel really scared when you talk to me like that, and
> I want you to stop."

The first remark is inflammatory. Angry action is threatened, tempting the other person to react in kind. And the temperature will continue to rise. With the second remark, the speaker may feel anger but is more detached and therefore able to be more in touch with a primary feeling: the fear that's driving the anger. Naming this deeper emotional reality is a powerful move. It invites the other person to join the speaker in lowering the temperature.

When we lack the personal authority to articulate what we most deeply want or feel, one of two outcomes is likely, both of them uncreative. First, we may unconsciously come on like a parent, commanding change, seeking control through some form of intimidation. Or second, we may flee the situation entirely (emotionally if not physically) in order to restore a sense of safety. In either event, we'll resort to behaviors that are ineffective, reactive, and off-center.

All of us can be knocked off center and out of our authority. There is no such thing as permanent residence in these wiser, more detached realms; we all can lose track of our deeper selves. It's a good idea, therefore, to identify the anxiety-ridden habitats of our own special demons.

Prone to feel blamed? If so, get ready for a ten-year-old self to materialize when only a faint shadow of blame lurks nearby. Worried about looking stupid? Watch the defensive lineman in us show up within seconds. Got a burning need to be right? Here comes our inner schoolmarm, smugly lunging for the dictionary or some other weapon, prompting inevitable eyeball-rolling from the person about to be skewered by righteous fervor.

Taking Things Personally

When we find ourselves seized by one of these demons from off center, we've usually flipped into taking things too personally—a mind-set already in play when a spat is gathering. Over-personalizing is the opposite of being detached, and there's one foolproof way to tell whether we're in its ferocious grip: a lost capacity to laugh at ourselves.

Taking things too personally, of course, means that besides losing our detachment, we are now engaged in propping up our sagging self-image. The only cure is to locate the self-deprecating laugh that lives somewhere in each of us. Think about being blamed for some wrongdoing that really wasn't our fault. When we can laugh and meet the blamer by immediately smacking ourselves in the forehead and exclaiming, "Oh, it's *so much worse* than you think," that's detachment. And at that moment, our over-personalizing evaporates.

It's sometimes said that there's an enormous belly laugh in the heart of God—not a laugh at us, as some fear, but a laugh with us. Earlier we suggested that the spiritual task was to find the belly laugh at the bottom of our own emotional well. Not taking things personally means we have found our way down into that deeper water.

Dealing with Our Flaws

One loud cautionary note needs to be registered here. We are only able to locate that belly laugh when we have realistic expectations of ourselves and can avoid the toxic perfectionism of the modern world. Ancient people knew they were flawed; only the gods were perfect. But in modern life we've now mostly lost this perspective on human flaws and that makes us easily seduced by perfectionism.

Perfectionism draws a particularly vicious circle around us. To whatever degree we expect ourselves to be flawless, criticism will feel threatening, and detachment will elude us. We will then have considerable trouble forgiving ourselves or anyone else. And in a further unpleasant irony, our perfectionism may drive us toward being very judgmental. Cutting ourselves precious little slack, we are likely to do the same to others, completing the circle of unforgiveness and judgment. Perfectionism may be invisible, but its consequences will ripple through our intimate relationships, making it difficult to throw our heads back in delighted laughter at our own idiocies.

Dark Corners

In forming realistic expectations of ourselves, we eventually have to reckon with flaws that we may not easily see but that others—especially our partners—can often identify with mortifying accuracy. These are the unattractive personality traits potentially present in all of us, a short list of which might include insensitivity, inability to apologize, emotional passivity, harshness, willfulness, self-absorption, and intrusiveness. If we tack on impatience, reactivity, disorganization, and obliviousness, our shadow side comes further into focus.

When we press on into even darker corners, looking for capacities we can all display sometimes, like manipulation, dishonesty, and even betrayal, it's plain that the list of flaws is not short at all but will be as long as the ragtag line of humanity itself. Yet if these flaws are so easy for others to spot but so difficult for us to acknowledge, how do we deal with them in an emotionally intimate relationship?

Fortunately, there's a straightforward and hopeful answer. While the flaws themselves are unappealing, we become enormously appealing by fully facing them. After all, who among us hasn't insisted on his or her own way, or heard merely what we want to hear, or "forgotten" something when remembering it was inconvenient? Honest self-assessment takes courage, and a partner whose listening spirit is tuned up will swiftly recognize our bravery.

Ultimately, the entire subject is a spiritual one. It's not enough to "understand" that we have certain blind spots or dark corners that need the light of day; we have to grapple with what we're going to *do* about them. What are we going to radically alter—"convert" is the right word—so that new life can spring up in a formerly dead place? If we can summon the humility not just to admit our failings but also to take responsibility for changing them, it usually leads to a bloom of respect in our partner and a surge of creative energy in the relationship.

Two Spiritual Decisions

Once we see our flaws more clearly, become more aware of the importance of detachment and personal authority, and acknowledge our anxieties, focus can shift toward making two spiritual decisions essential to a passionate relationship. We call them decisions rather than skills because they require a cold-light-of-day realization by the speaker that these are choices. They don't happen by accident. Furthermore, they are choices we make to maintain our own integrity, regardless of what our partner does.

The Decision to Speak Respectfully

This is a spiritual decision that's difficult to make and keep, in part because many of us have not grown up experiencing being spoken *to* respectfully. Think of a man whose siblings and parents were all masters at the art of hurling one-liners, often laced with sarcasm. Not only does this become a well-learned pattern of communicating, but it may also seem completely normal—until a partner enters the scene and says that it feels like an advanced form of verbal warfare. In time, the man may come to realize that there was indeed a short supply of respectful talk around his original dinner table.

Although the decision to speak respectfully might occasionally force us to bite our tongue, it's an integral part of emotional intimacy, because our partner comes to count on it and eventually relaxes into it. Respectful speaking is tied up with emotional safety and feeling invited to reveal our vulnerabilities. The family just described is far from "safe"; everyone's foibles and tender spots are in the crosshairs. There may be plenty of laughter, but it's often laughter at, not with, as though family members are playing a sly game of Gotcha. Fortunately, a sincere effort to speak respectfully with an intimate partner can eventually remove fear of verbal land mines and heal much of the damage sustained from these earlier, emotionally confusing experiences.

Once we become confident that we can speak (and will be spoken to) respectfully, a strange thing begins to happen: we discover that we can express what we want and feel where we were previously tongue-tied. This applies even to difficult topics—perhaps especially to them. We can be angry, for example, and if we express it early and respectfully, we will harness our anger long before it has a chance to boil over. Even in hot emotional moments, respectful speaking has the potential to stop a spat from turning into a fight.

Obviously, we can't always manage to pull this off; we will sometimes fall back into being disrespectful. But if we can return our sights to the prior commitment we've made, we'll restore our original intention faster. This much is clear: the old childhood rhyme, "Sticks and stones may break my bones, but names will never hurt me," simply isn't true. If we work at it long enough, disrespectful talk can do mortal damage and destroy any chance for emotional intimacy.

The Decision to Not Become Defensive

Dubious as it may sound, and despite the spiritual discipline needed to pull it off, nothing keeps a spat more firmly in line than deciding not to become defensive. Every time, in every case, until defanged, defensiveness will send a spat off the known map and into fighting territory. Hear the following exchange through the lens of that claim:

> Lisa: "You *never* help around the house!"
> Mike: "I do too!"

In a moment of real life, Mike would very likely go on, with raised voice, to list all the ways he frequently helps, conclusively demonstrating his defensiveness. He might claim he's simply setting the record straight, and maybe he is, but his defensiveness stains the conversation like a leaky pen.

Defensiveness begins when we lose our detachment and experience anxiety from feeling under attack. Defensiveness is further fed by the illusion that if we offer counter-arguments, we will change the other person's perspective, halt the attack, and maybe even win an apology. This rarely happens; just look at Lisa. Her view might shift slightly to "Okay, you do take out the garbage once in a while," but her original criticism of his "never helping around the house" doesn't budge. In fact, her criticism may get louder and larger.

When absolute words like "never" and "always" come through the door, it's a sign that all defensive armor should be laid down. This is very hard to do, since we're likely to feel we *are* under attack. Yet the swiftest way to stop a fight in its tracks is to listen to the accuser's feelings—including the absolutes—and invite him or her to tell us fully about those feelings. That's just what Bill did in chapter 5, when Jeanne entered his office wrapped in an emotional fit. Bill didn't resort to defensiveness but instead asked Jeanne to tell him what her anger was about.

In the effort to become non-defensive, each of us could profitably memorize and then practice the following words: "Just because someone is mad at me doesn't mean I've done anything wrong." Engraving this on our hearts will help maintain our detachment. Otherwise, when an accusation of wrongdoing lands on us (often flooding us with a strong dose of fear), most of us will tip instantly into the primitive reaction of defensiveness. Instead, we need to figure out how to remain calm—just as Bill did with Jeanne—and stay rooted in as much empathetic separateness as we can find. Despite the knee-jerk quality to defensiveness, we *can* learn to stop doing it. The following steps are simple. They also require determined perseverance to become distilled into habits.

First of all, again, we have to quiet our anxiety. At the start, this probably means a willingness to be silent—perhaps only for a minute but maybe for the time required to go on a brief walk. However long it takes, we need to find genuine quiet within us. Second, in this period of quieting down we need to remind ourselves: defensiveness doesn't work in an intimate relationship. It will inevitably backfire and enflame the situation. If we can slow down, take a deep breath, and let our heads take the lead, defensiveness has a chance to abate. Finally, we need to summon our curiosity, full force, and attend to what our partner is trying to communicate. The simple invitation to "tell me more" is often the best response in a heated moment. If spoken without sarcasm and with true empathetic curiosity, these words will win respect and open many an emotional door.

Because it's so difficult to actually achieve this non-defensiveness, we're best off with acknowledging how often we fail at it. Just like the failure to speak respectfully, we will still get defensive, especially when caught off guard by some threatening comment. All we can do at that point is acknowledge our defensiveness, and begin again. Although gaining success with this second spiritual decision may feel painfully slow, if it's our serious intent, it will eventually come into focus— like a photographic negative that's spent enough time in the developing solution.

A Shift in Vision

When the many aspects of the speaker's spirit described in this chapter are working together, a new vision for relating to our partner appears on the horizon. This shift does involve definite skills on the part of the speaker, yet when just the spirit alone is in place, the emotional ground of the relationship begins to change. To whatever extent we were caught in a narrow, anxious, win/lose perspective, we can now adopt a much wider win/win perspective, which makes an intense difference in how we love someone. To illustrate:

- We can imagine standing up to a partner where we need to and *also* happily surrender when we know a partner's perspective is more on target than our own.
- We can imagine speaking non-defensively and *also* find the curiosity to explore what our partner is disturbed about.
- We can imagine fully expressing our own feelings and needs, and *also* hear our partner's feelings and needs as equally valid.

In other words, we trade in those aspects of our relationship that are anxious and competitive, and receive in return shared authority and mutual vulnerability. Vulnerability here doesn't mean weak or enfeebled; it's the opposite. This vulnerability is strong and resilient. It's about being real. It involves speaking boldly about whatever emotional truth we're experiencing, and feeling empowered.

Returning to Mike and Lisa in their tussle over the housework, this same empowering vision will open up for them if Mike lets his defensiveness go and focuses instead on Lisa's feelings. If he makes himself vulnerable to whatever kernel of truth her feelings reveal, he will earn her respect and trigger her forgiveness.

At the same time, Mike needs to tell Lisa that her initial bark at him, "You never help with the housework!" felt judgmental and hurtful—not exactly an invitation to non-defensiveness. When Lisa acknowledges Mike's feelings and her own poor approach, they will be able to move toward a creative spat that might begin resolving a very old beef. To do that, both people need a strong speaker's spirit and real skills. We turn now to those skills.

This above all, to refuse to be a victim. Unless I can do that
I can do nothing. I have to recant, give up the old belief
that I am powerless.

Margaret Atwood

CHAPTER 8

Learn the Skills Needed for Emotionally Intimate Conversation

Keep Listening

The first daunting task we all face in any oncoming spat is how to prevent our speaking from eclipsing our continued listening. And we mean listening at multiple levels. For example:

A man and woman are having a conversation that threatens to slide into tense territory. At some point, while he is talking, her eyes start to darken and register disturbance. A nerve in her has been touched. Unless the man notices this, listens to it, and asks what she's feeling, any intimate connection between them will break, even though the conversation may well go forward.

Moments like this pose an uncomfortable question to the speaker: if someone's eyes are glazing over—whether from distress, boredom, or perplexity—why are we continuing to talk? Once we've finished our thought, we need to invite the other person to articulate what we've sensed in his or her eyes, body language, or words. The first speaking skill we have to develop, then, if we want a passionately intimate life, requires finely tuned antennae to discern when to stop speaking. It's all about embracing quiet to a degree that can feel very new.

Mastering Silence

The initial step in "going quiet," when it's called for, lies in mastering silence and learning to sit with our feelings before we speak. Feelings sometimes require time to sort out, letting the truest of them (perhaps the most nuanced) rise to the surface.

If ideas get tossed back and forth too fast in a conversation, especially a tense one, our feelings tend to run together and leap anxiously out of us. They usually take shape as some form of reactive talk—overstatement, blame, exaggeration, "judgmentalness"—any of which will whip up the waters of a spat. But when we can speak slowly or stop for a moment, our feelings have time to distill. Focusing on our own interior experience, we have a chance of quieting down. This quiet allows us to hear ourselves during a rush of feeling and to get clearer about what we want to say.

Becoming intentional this way is a deliberate attempt to be extra-conscious. It's different from what happens during normal, everyday conversation, when super-sharp awareness often isn't necessary. But a looming spat needs to bring on heightened consciousness in order to keep it from mutating into a fight.

Another step in mastering silence, and getting past anxious talk, requires a conscious decision to stop talking when we don't feel heard. If a partner becomes distracted by a task, a thought, or a ringing telephone when a spat is in the air, just stop talking. At that point, our partner isn't listening anymore, even if they think they are. And if we keep talking when someone isn't listening, we're just reinforcing a kind of pseudo-attention in the relationship. Modern life may work squarely against getting someone's undivided attention, but that's what a successful spat requires—no distraction. Unless we can give each other our full attention, we won't get anywhere in resolving whatever issue is plaguing us at the moment.

Exactly Why Are We Talking Anyway?

We also need to become aware of what's prompting us to speak in the first place. Think back to some occasion, like a committee meeting, where a person seemed to be talking mostly to hear the sound of his or her own voice. Who among us hasn't occasionally done that? We're all capable of filling space with yak because we're uncomfortable or simply to remind ourselves that we exist. Yet this can amount to little more than anxious prattle.

Quakers have an old and useful practice called "speaking out of the silence," which means just that: intentional silence undergirding equally intentional speaking. In a secular setting, it might work as follows:

A small group of people is having a contentious conversation that's on the verge of erupting into a firestorm of controversy and argument. The facilitator, aware of the anxiety flying around the room, suggests adopting a new approach. He asks everyone to locate a zone of real silence within themselves, and to speak only from there. Additionally, the group agrees that fifteen seconds of silence will separate speakers. This purposeful speaking, alternated with periodic silences, produces a dramatic result. Deep, deliberative quiet spreads slowly through the group, and a thoughtful, productive conversation unfolds.

Whether in a group setting or an intimate relationship, the same issue needs to be addressed—determining if our talk is coming from the wise person within us or from the nervous natterer wanting to get heard. To discern which is which, we can listen to the speed at which we're speaking and to how often we interrupt. Rapid speaking and the impulse to interrupt are almost always fed by some measure of anxiety, whatever its multiple sources may be.

Much of the talk in an intimate relationship is pleasurable and spontaneous. Heightened consciousness isn't then the point; a relaxed spirit of companionship is. But when tension rises, we need to get very clear and conscious about what's moving us to speak. If we want to avoid the anxious trivialities that will derail a spat, one or more of the following needs to be our purpose:

- to express empathy for our partner
- to ask what our partner is feeling
- to reveal our own feelings and their effect on us
- to share helpful information, pertinent to the spat at hand
- to be supportive
- to tell our partner how his or her behavior is affecting us
- to confront

In a spat, we have to acknowledge that there's business at hand; some issue needs to be talked through, resolved, finished, and let go. This requires willingness to stick to the point and engage in purposeful talk. Moreover, it means sensing what's relevant to a particular conversation. While all the reasons for speaking listed above are valid, what's most important is what's most immediate. In other words, what needs to be said now, in this moment.

The Art of the Question

A necessary—and often overlooked—speaking skill lies in knowing how to pose penetrating questions that invite revealing answers. Too often, we ask questions that leave a partner's deeper emotional experience untouched, failing to increase the emotional intimacy in a relationship. A simple example will demonstrate this art:

He: "I talked to my dad today."

She: "Was it a good conversation?"

He: "It was okay."

She: "How was he?"

He: (pauses) "Depressed."

She: "Do you want to talk about it?"

He: "You already know the story."

She: "I know how conversations with him sometimes leave you feeling. How did you feel this time?"

He: "I don't know."

She waits without speaking; her full attention turned to him.

He: "I'm so confused. It's hard for me, not knowing how to help my dad."

It often takes a brief, patient interlude before a person disturbed about something will be able to talk about it. The woman's capacity here to stick with quiet, inviting questions allows them both to reach the outskirts of an intimate conversation.

We can get skilled at the art of asking good questions by figuring out:

- how often we ask follow-up questions
- whether we continue to refine our understanding of a situation or too quickly accept superficial answers

- whether we allow a partner time to descend to a fuller range of his or her feelings

This really boils down to one question: how much curiosity can we summon on our partner's behalf? If we're honest about it, many of us are able to drum up only half-hearted curiosity—and often, not even that. We're preoccupied, busy, distracted, self-concerned, and find it hard to tap the energy that is curiosity's lifeblood. Given this probable lukewarmness, it's worth remembering that *curiosity* is one of the words etched above the gateway into a passionately intimate life.

The Speaking That Love Demands

While we may not normally think of the words "love" and "demand" as belonging in the same sentence, they share an important connection. Especially during a spat. If our goal is to build emotional bridges, we have to be open to an ancient spiritual prescription for human relationships, which is learning to speak the truth in love.

Speaking the truth in love places at least the following demands on us: giving, receiving, maintaining our separateness, and confronting when necessary. Giving and receiving are the most attractive and obvious of love's demands. We assume both must happen to define a relationship as "loving," and nearly all of us engage these twin aspects of love with delight.

Love's demands for separateness and confrontation are much harder to meet, in part because they feel contradictory to the way we think of love. Each involves standing our ground and maintaining our independence, particularly during an emotionally difficult exchange. For example, we may love a partner very much. But when we feel our boundaries have somehow been crossed, love bids us to speak up, to stay true to ourselves, and to maintain our integrity about what we think and feel. Subtle interior whisperings can tempt us to ignore a crossed boundary or to change some aspect of ourselves just to keep the peace; most of us hate to see the peace disturbed. Real emotional intimacy, however, extracts a distinct price here. We have to stand on our own separate piece of ground when necessary.

This means, of course, that confrontation lives right outside the door. It doesn't go away; it just goes to sleep. And it's always ready to spring up at a moment's notice. Even though we resist the idea of confronting someone we love, it's unrealistic to imagine that confrontation isn't occasionally required to keep the relationship on track. It is. The choice of peace at any price simply buries unresolved issues, stockpiles resentment, and eventually returns to haunt us. Spats are precisely intended to reduce our fear of confrontation, thereby preventing necessary struggles from turning into unnecessary fights.

A long way back, we remarked that for many of us, love and anger seem irreconcilable. But when a burr sits under our emotional saddle, skillfully "speaking the truth in love" is important in expressing anger appropriately. This is the case, for instance, when we're concerned about a partner's well-being or about some aspect of the relationship.

Regarding a partner's well-being, the operative word is probably danger. If we sense danger in a certain behavior, (overworking, drinking too much, eating recklessly), then a commitment to speaking the truth in love compels us to bring the matter up.

Likewise, when we're concerned about some sort of disturbance in the relationship, love insists that we speak of it. Such disturbance could be relatively mild, such as, "We're not getting much time together," or, more troubling, "It has been forever since we last made love." Whatever the magnitude of discomfort felt, the truth of it needs to be spoken, in love, or the relationship's intimacy will be diminished. As someone once said, unless we're speaking the truth to one another, it's not a relationship—it's an arrangement.

Developing the Skills to Lovingly Confront

In order to understand how a successful, loving confrontation unfolds, recall the points we made earlier about the speaker's spirit. We said it was crucial to maintain separateness, detachment, and firmness in our own personal authority, all with an eye toward reducing defensiveness. Granted, that's a lot to manage simultaneously. But intentionally realigning our spirit will make it much easier to master the following confrontation skills:

A Slow, Soft Start

First, we need to do everything possible to begin with a soft entry, one that's deliberately tentative yet names our own desire as straightforwardly as possible. For example:

> "I'd like to talk with you about something that's
> bothering me."
>
> vs.

"I'm sick and tired of the way you're treating the kids.
You have to change."

The soft approach amounts to starting slowly and without a lot of heavy breathing. If we need to talk about difficult things with a partner, we have to allow him or her time to come up to speed and get on board with us. It won't work if we leap in and start slinging accusations all around the room; we'll just plug our partner's ears. And we'll also trigger defensiveness. Making a low-key beginning enables us to clear the way for unexaggerated disclosure of how we're feeling and what's troubling us.

Always Two Sides
Second, we stand the best chance of starting a spat gently if we first remind ourselves, in quadruplicate, that during any confrontation between two intimately related people, there are always two sides to be explored. Always. We may be too fired up to see the other side, but it's there. And unless we make it clear that we are *speaking solely from our own point of view*, we'll provoke immediate resistance to what we're trying to say.

Accordingly, when talking about whatever is awry between us at the moment, it's important to use a phrase like "my experience is," rather than appointing ourselves Bearer of the One Truth. By acknowledging (without secret disdain) that a certain accounting of events is just our own perception, our own version, we make room for a different point of view— theirs. Too often, we say that another truth exists but don't really believe it. We have to believe it.

Allowing for more than one side also means getting skilled at recognizing when we haven't done that. Claiming a hard-

and-fast position is disturbing and likely to make a partner feel marooned, feisty, and wounded, all at the same time. If we can take swift responsibility, admit the fault, apologize, and throttle down, we can create the necessary space to begin again.

Beware of Fighting Words

The third confrontation skill involves living into the prior commitment to speak respectfully and rejecting certain behaviors as completely out of bounds—like sarcasm, shaming, blaming, name-calling, and mocking. All put-down speech, consciously or not, causes pain and intends to puncture a partner's self-esteem. It also reveals one underlying aim: gaining emotional leverage in an argument. Whether such blunt weapons deliver "victory" at some crude level is beside the point. As suggested earlier, they do enormous damage. They also invariably spark defensiveness, eventually overwhelming even a mature partner's desire to stay open and remain non-defensive. And of course, use of these weapons diminishes the person wielding them.

In order to make good on our intention to speak respectfully, we have to be fully conscious of our feelings and stay in charge of them. Otherwise, we'll just get caught in their grip. A person resorting to mockery or a barrage of sarcasm has been kidnapped by his or her feelings and rendered unable to speak creatively. In every instance, it's emotionally more powerful when we can just state our feelings, without exaggeration or drama, rather than stooping to skewering the other person.

Abstaining from put-down speech is one side of the equation; the other is what to do if we're on the receiving end of it. Since we need to demand the respect from our partner that we are trying to exhibit ourselves, the best response is the simplest. Just name the out-of-bounds behavior and refuse to continue any conversation until it stops. Completely. To work, this has to be done when we hear the first echoes of a put-down. If we wait until we're verging on white-hot mad, we'll be tempted to cause injury that matches the injury we feel ourselves.

Put-downs can be subtle. But even oblique expressions of disdain will be plenty corrosive to the intimacy in a relationship. For instance:

> A husband with long-standing weight problems promises himself that this time he's really going to make a diet work, and he confides his hopes to his wife. He sticks to his plan for about ten days, and then she comes upon him one afternoon shoveling large spoonfuls of ice cream into his mouth. "I thought you wanted to lose weight," she says.

Comments like this amount to not-so-thinly-veiled shaming. They are also intrusive, holding a partner's feet to the fire when we haven't been invited to do that. While there are many potential responses to someone who has fallen off the diet wagon, shaming in any form isn't one of them.

Timing

In the face of a spat, usually because we're anxious about the subject at hand and have sat too long on our feelings, we can demonstrate an uncanny sense of poor timing. But as a speaker, it's important to determine whether the present moment is auspicious. We classically underestimate how much time will be required to engage a spat, let alone to finish it, and these miscalculations sabotage the spat's chance for success. Too often, we'll blurt something out, or insist on an immediate discussion, or force a subject into too narrow a time slot. If someone has just come home from a long day's work, though, the timing doesn't bode well for taking up a prickly issue. Similarly, we're likely to fare poorly if we raise a serious subject on our way out the door, or ten minutes before hungry children tumble into the kitchen looking for supper.

Though we can be dim at recognizing how faulty our sense of timing is, we can also avoid these timing traps quite easily. When our partner is arriving from work, we need to allow some space for getting re-acclimated to being home. This isn't manipulative; it's just wise. We also need to ask whether this particular moment is a good time to talk. If the response doesn't match our own desires, we have to back up. This is another aspect of making a slow entry. All of us prefer a little headroom and a chance to agree with the timing of a conversation, before jumping into choppy water.

There is one glaring exception to the foregoing: a person consistently wanting to avoid talking about something and for whom there is never a "good" time. Promises keep getting made to engage a subject but mysteriously, the right moment never materializes. In this case, the other partner has little choice but to plant a foot in the ever-closing conversational door and insist the avoider set a time that *will* work.

Focusing on One Issue

When a spat is imminent, we need the skill of keeping only one issue on the table at a time. This may seem easy, but it can be very tricky. Consider this exchange:

> Woman: "I'd like to talk about my unhappiness with the way you spoke to my mother."

> Man: "I don't like the way you treat my family either."

The man's response might sound as though he is speaking to the point, but actually he introduces a new issue and is defensive to boot. In a creative spat, whoever raises a particular concern needs to be confident that a partner is willing to stay with that subject until it's talked through. When we're being confronted, however, we're often powerfully tempted to shift the ground. If we're told that someone is unhappy with us, it puts us on the spot and spikes our anxiety. Despite this anxiety, we have to let the focus of the spat remain on our partner's feelings until real satisfaction is gained, rather than switching to our own concerns. We can't use the occasion to bring up some grievance we've been nursing, even if it seems related. Instead, it's a moment for expanding our commitment to listen.

Focus on Feelings, Not on Information

In many instances, we hope to sidestep a spat by giving out information rather than revealing our feelings. For example:

> A young woman is balking at the idea of going to her husband's family farm for Christmas. She tells him, "I really don't want to go" [information]. Queried by her husband, she says, "There's nothing to do at the farm [information]. I'm a city girl anyway [information]. Your mother is always busy when we visit [information], and your brothers come around but only to do chores with you and your father" [information]. Pressed further, she finally admits, "I'm afraid [feelings] your mother doesn't really like me. I'm embarrassed [feelings] because I don't know how to be helpful. And you go off with your father and brothers so often to do jobs around the farm that I end up anxious and lonely" [feelings].

When we as speakers only cite information, about farms or anything else, it creates distance from our partner because we are talking *around* a subject rather than being direct about how we feel. There are many circumstances in which we offer little except information—and deliberately so. Think of a cocktail party. We share information galore, and it's almost exclusively small talk. Indeed, it's considered bad form to steer the conversation into territory too intense or personal.

In contrast, the intent of an intimate relationship is to be visible, to be emotionally present. And we achieve that by speaking about our feelings, not by peering out from behind a thick curtain of information. Couples can be startled to realize that although they spend copious amounts of time trading facts, making plans, and sharing information about who's going to pick up which child at which activity, it may have been a long, lonely time since they really talked to one another about all the feelings underneath the busyness of their lives. Because those unexpressed feelings can eventually become the kindling for a fight, it's no wonder we often just stick with imparting information. It's invariably safer, if dependably dull.

Brevity is the Soul of Wit . . . and of Intimacy

A crucial speaking skill, particularly in emotionally vulnerable conversations, is the ability to be brief, direct, and specific. If we string together more than a few sentences at a time, we will pass over the border of conversation, and enter the country of soliloquy and monologue. The archenemies of intimacy live here. Coming right to the point about our feelings *is* the point, and yet how often we don't do that.

Lots of us suffer from a distinct flaw in regard to brevity: we repeat ourselves. Exactly why we do is all bound up with anxiety and our level of discomfort with silence. A few factors, sometimes in combination, are usually behind our repeating. For one thing, we may think that the other person didn't get exactly what we meant, so we go over it again, perhaps with minor changes but not substantively altering what we said. Or if we're looking for agreement and sense disagreement coming, we'll double back and repeat ourselves, hoping that our re-emphasizing will change the picture. Finally, if we're anxious about silence, and our partner doesn't respond fast enough, the silence may drive us to keep blatting away, placing brevity on the casualty list.

The opposite behavior needs to become a well-sharpened arrow in the speaker's quiver. We have to get good at succinctly saying our piece, get even better at waiting in silence as our partner takes our words in, and continue to be receptively silent while our partner is thinking about what to say. While this might sound wooden, in practice it will keep a spat from metastasizing.

Loaded Language

Although we may be largely unaware of it, the language we use in a conversation can come out heavily seasoned with exaggeration, judgment, and innuendo. Absolute phrases like "you always" and "you never" are common examples of loaded language and will drive a partner's back up for a couple of reasons. For starters, most of us don't "always" or "never" do any particular thing, and if we pigeonhole a person this way, he's going to bristle. Additionally, absolutes erase any sense of tentativeness, suggesting that the speaker is fixed solely on his or her own point of view. Speaking in absolutes also carries a strong whiff of competitiveness and impending argument, further lessening the likelihood that any genuine listening will happen.

It's difficult to discern the way loaded language works in intimate relationships because the culture at large is so thoroughly infected with it—to the point that we may be numb to its effects. Think of a phrase like "tax-and-spend liberals." Whether spoken or printed, the words are dripping with disdain, implying a supposed "truth" whose meaning is fixed for all time. It's no different when loaded language creeps into intimate conversation. It's the language of judgment, closed thinking, and hardened hearts, and it's as corrosive in the private sphere as in the public one.

Changing "But" into "And"

The simple word "but" is an illustration of how we can subtly load language. Obviously, "but" is used constantly to make all sorts of necessary distinctions. However, in intimate relationships (if there's some measure of tension afoot), when we use "but" as the hinge of a sentence, the second half of the sentence is likely to contain a veiled criticism. For example:

> "I forgive you, but we haven't worked through what happened."

> "I like your haircut, but he should have cut it shorter."

These comments are loaded because they garble the truth. Forgiveness hasn't really occurred, and the haircut needs help. When we're unable to articulate the full truth or don't want to sound openly critical, we connect the two halves of a sentence with "but," imagining that a positive beginning will alter a negative end. It won't. These sentences can be unloaded by amplifying them with more of the truth and changing "but" to "and":

> "I really want to forgive you, and we need to work through what happened."

"I like your haircut, and it also seems to me to be a little long."

If this feels like an absurdly small change to make in one's speaking, it is. And listening to see how frequently it crops up will deliver an absurdly large payoff, in part because the person digesting a "but" often senses that a slice of untruthfulness has just been served up.

Hidden Damage

Loaded language increases alienation and feeds fights; the remark from the wife to her ice cream-eating husband about his "wanting to lose weight" is one such example. Despite being oblique and seemingly casual, it's packing plenty of punch and can function like a tiny emotional hand grenade.

Loaded language damages relationships. Such language makes it hard to trust that a partner will give an accurate, even-handed description of difficult moments. For instance, if we make the loaded comment, "It's impossible to talk to you!" we may believe we are only stating the obvious. Not so. Hyperbole like this is an attempt to overwhelm someone with our "rightness." But it won't work. The opposite will happen, and the other person will simply be convinced of how impossible it is to talk to *us*.

All full-blown arguments are laden with bombast and overstatement—it's their hallmark. When we are able to unload our language, however, we can back down from the noisy polarization of an argument into the quieter regions of a spat. If we can speak calmly, without exaggeration, our partner will be able to believe that he or she will receive fairness from us and will more readily ungird his or her own loins.

Speak for Yourself

As speakers we need to develop the laser-sharp skill of talking only for ourselves and about our own feelings, rather than assuming what someone else thinks or feels and then talking for that person.

To gauge how adept we are at speaking just for ourselves, try the simple test of listening for how often our sentences begin with the word "you," instead of the word "I," particularly in anxious moments. When the fur is in danger of flying, use of the pronoun "you" will raise someone's hackles—and reasonably so, because it's judgmental interpreting of that person's behavior. Starting a sentence with the word "you" guarantees that whatever follows will be our fantasy of someone else's thoughts and feelings. For instance, a husband says to his wife:

> "You must not want me to be a part of things. You don't talk to me before making plans with the kids."

His words reveal how much assuming he's doing; he has no idea what's actually behind his wife's behavior. Maybe she perceives him as terribly busy and is compassionately trying to take the pressure off him. Or maybe her father always expected her mother to make plans for the kids, and she thinks this is just the way things are supposed to be. Maybe he's right, and she's avoiding him. But he doesn't know any of this. He's assuming he knows.

The same exchange gets significantly altered if the man speaks only for himself:

"I find it upsetting and painful when you don't talk with me before making plans with the kids."

She isn't likely to become defensive if her husband simply expresses his own feelings. To be sure, he makes himself much more vulnerable when he talks about himself, and that's the point. In a passionate relationship, speaking only for ourselves will inevitably increase our vulnerability. This risk-taking, in turn, pushes open the door to expanded emotional intimacy.

Think of this another way. Recall responding with suppressed agitation when someone says, "I know how you feel." They don't know, and they can't. No one knows how we feel, because no one lives inside us. The job we each have in an intimate relationship is to bravely reveal our own experience, our own feelings, so that our partner isn't reduced to speculation. Many of us need to learn to speak up—usually much faster than we are prone to—and when we do, whatever we're saying needs to be about our own experience.

Speaking a Rounder Emotional Truth

Back in the chapters on listening, we talked about having multiple feelings simultaneously and learning to listen to the many nuances in those feelings. Here, a similar point applies to our speaking. In any moment (knowing all moments contain a host of feelings), we need to try to speak of them as fully as possible. Focusing on only a single feeling distorts our own emotional awareness and skews a partner's perception of what we're feeling.

For instance, if a husband is annoyed with his wife, and they enter into a conversation, his expressing the feelings he has *besides* annoyance will create a much rounder emotional reality. Even though he's annoyed, he can also tell her he's happy she's willing to talk, and he's anxious they might not get to the bottom of the difficulty, and he sympathizes in some measure with her point of view. Speaking in this fuller way is not only much closer to the speaker's own emotional experience but also tends to open the ears of the other person. We are complex beings. And we are far more likely to listen intently when someone reveals a corresponding complexity in his or her own emotional awareness.

If we only speak of our feelings one-dimensionally, the connection we make with our partner is much weaker. Getting stuck on just one feeling (like sadness, or fear, or empathy, or irritation) tends to mask the other feelings we're experiencing, causing us to lose touch with them. Think of catching a baseball. If we reach for it with only one finger, we'll surely drop it. But if we catch it roundly with our whole hand, we'll connect with it firmly. A similar rounded grasp in our feeling life brings nuanced emotional richness to a relationship and to a spat. If a wide range of feelings is accessible and is also expressed, we begin to realize that we can experience being angry *and* sad, angry *and* empathetic, grieved *and* relieved, scared *and* hopeful . . . or any other paradoxical combination of emotions.

Resolutions—True and False

Finally, both speakers in a spat need to stay with it until it's fully resolved. Exceptions are a spat that gets too hot and has to be stopped in mid-boil, or one requiring more than a single conversation. In those situations, both partners need to agree to call a momentary halt, and then return to the subject. Quickly, if possible.

There's a definitive way to tell whether true resolution of a spat has occurred: both partners will experience new sensitivity to one another and will feel closer. In addition, new understanding will emerge about whatever sparked the problem. It doesn't matter what the dispute is; every dispute needs a thorough enough airing so that both people feel satisfied.

Unfortunately, most of us are tempted to quit too soon. We press our case only until we experience momentary emotional relief, tricking ourselves into imagining that this shallow resolution means things are fixed. They aren't. Settling for a shallow resolution simply means that unresolved feelings will fester, waiting to spring back out in another guise. Since we can bank on unresolved trouble rearing its ugly head—every time—tackling that prospect merits its own separate chapter.

"If we want to claim the essential emotional part of our lives and reignite our passion and purpose, we have to learn how to . . . engage with our vulnerability and how to feel the emotions that come with it."

Brené Brown

CHAPTER 9

Insist on Getting to the Bottom of Trouble

Uncovering the Wound

Finding the bottom of a spat and genuinely resolving whatever thorny issue is on the table is, first and last, a matter of finding the wound—or wounds—that caused the spat to occur. "Wound" is the right word. In every spat, someone has been injured; sometimes, both people have. The wounds may be small, unintentional, or unconsciously caused, or there may be a misunderstanding. It doesn't make any difference. In order to arrive at a resolution, those wounds have to be named, cleaned out, and bandaged with believable care. Anything short of this will lead to continued soreness, as surely as will removal of only half a splinter.

The principal instrument for lancing an emotional wound is, of course, listening—and more important, listening to feelings. We've observed that disputing the facts in a contentious moment is futile. Everyone's facts are simply a point of view, driven by feelings. But when we stop debating the facts and let the wound be the primary lens, the chance for effective listening is vastly increased and the bottom of the spat comes into view much faster.

Before any helpful listening can occur, one prior move is necessary. The injured partner has to be able to name—with real clarity and relative calm—how she feels (e.g., i.e., sad, anxious, hurt, scared). She also needs to describe the specific behavior that left her wounded, but the feelings are the point. At the onset of a spat, it can be difficult to name the feelings because the wounded person may be too overwrought for articulate talk. Injured feelings often need to be coaxed out, letting them cool off and come into focus.

Bill and Jeanne Revisited

Fleshing out the encounter between Bill and Jeanne (in chapter 5) will illuminate the process of using feelings as the lens. Keeping track of the turning points in their conversation, the route they take to the bottom becomes evident.

Jeanne makes the wound obvious when she storms into Bill's office. Realizing immediately that listening to her feelings is the only creative approach, Bill sits down and starts to do just that:

Bill: "Please tell me why you're so angry."

Jeanne: "Because you shot your mouth off to my sister."

Bill is silent.

Jeanne: "You talked to her about our marriage!"

Bill remains silent.

Jeanne: "You did! Didn't you?"

Bill doesn't try to stop Jeanne from being angry. He stays concerned but detached, resisting his impulse to be defensive. By remaining quiet at first, he invites Jeanne to slow her rant and attempt to begin a conversation.

Bill: "I did talk to your sister."

Jeanne: "Well, you had no right. I feel totally betrayed."

Bill: "I'm sorry you feel betrayed."

Jeanne is quiet for a moment.

The **first turning point** occurs when Bill's empathy begins to register with Jeanne. Rational conversation becomes a possibility. As Bill is able to hear into the hurt under Jeanne's anger and empathize with her, she can begin to stop being reactive and start being responsive. Note: Bill's empathy doesn't mean he accepts blame for the situation.

Bill: "I do think we need to fully talk through what happened. What have you been told?"

Jeanne: "I'd rather hear it from your side."

Bill is curious to find out what specific responsibility Jeanne thinks he should take. However, hearing the suspicion in Jeanne's voice that he might select facts that shield him from taking responsibility, Bill willingly speaks first.

Bill: "When your sister called me, concerned about both of us, I did talk to her."

Jeanne: "I can't believe you talked to her about us."

Bill: "Actually, you don't know what happened in the conversation."

Bill stands his ground in pointing out that Jeanne is assuming more than she knows. He is simultaneously working to hang onto his empathy and keep any self-righteous or competitive tone out of his voice.

Jeanne: "Well, what did you say?"

Bill: "I thanked her for her concern, and acknowledged only what she already knows: that we're stressed. Beyond that, I suggested she talk to you."

Jeanne: "She told me you talked about my temper!"

Bill: "We did. She brought it up and was expressing worry. I gave her no new information. I did say that I was pretty concerned myself."

Bill's brief, non-inflammatory response to Jeanne's remark gives her some room to reflect. If he'd gone on at length or tried to justify himself, it would have only increased Jeanne's anger and reduced her trust.

Jeanne: "I feel as though you were disloyal to me."

Bill: "I can really understand that."

Jeanne: "Great. It's a little late."

Bill: "I'm very sorry about all this, Jeanne."

Almost predictably, Jeanne has been stung anew by the incident and is unable to let it go yet. Bill maintains his empathy while he continues to try to penetrate why she feels betrayed.

Bill: "Let's talk about what actually happened in my conversation with your sister. I need to understand more about how you think I was disloyal to you."

Jeanne: "You shouldn't have talked to her."

Bill: "But she was the one who called me. What do you think I should have said?"

Jeanne: "How about, 'Our marriage is none of your business'?"

Bill: "That's true. But does it seem real that I would come on so defensively in response to a phone call from a family member expressing concern about us? She did sound very genuine."

Jeanne: "Well, no . . . I can see you were trying to be polite."

Bill: "Yes, and I was also caught off guard."

Jeanne: "I get that."

Bill does a couple of helpful things here. First, he asks gently challenging questions that invite Jeanne to focus on her assumptions about what he did, and whether he did it so badly. (Arguing with her to get her to hear his point of view will just shove the spat into fighting mode.) Second, he puts himself under her scrutiny, so she is free to decide whether he really was disloyal to her.

Bill: "Besides, a part of me was glad she called, even though I had to restrain myself."

Jeanne: "What did you say to her?"

Bill: "As best I can remember, the conversation lasted about five minutes. She did most of the talking—all of it about you—and it was focused on your sometimes excessive anger. I tried my best not to join her in her criticism and made it clear I wasn't blameless in all this."

Bill takes some risks. He acknowledges to Jeanne that he was both human enough to be relieved to talk and had to resist teaming up with the criticism of her. When he tells Jeanne's sister that he isn't blameless, Bill's awareness of his own culpability functions to support Jeanne.

Jeanne: "The whole thing pisses me off."

Bill: "Okay. But what I'm curious to know is what you're holding me accountable for."

Jeanne: "She should never have called you."

Bill: "But she did."

Jeanne: "You should never have talked to her."

Bill: "That may be easy to say after the fact. Do you really blame me for my handling of *her* call, which caught me off guard?"

Jeanne: "Well, I suppose not."

Bill: "Suppose?"

Jeanne: "No . . . it stings me, though, to think she was able to draw you into talking about me behind my back."

Bill: "I realize that. And I'm really sorry it happened. I did only an okay job with the conversation. Next time, I think I'd end it quickly and graciously instead of managing so carefully what I said. Now I feel kind of annoyed with myself about talking to her in the first place."

This is the **second turning point** in the spat. Bill's empathy is maintained alongside his taking responsibility, and Jeanne sees that he made some mistakes, but never intended to wound her. While the word forgiveness hasn't been directly spoken yet, she is now in the process of forgiving him. The goodwill is also restored enough to reach down a little further.

Jeanne: "I have to admit that I'm fearful about my sister's ability to drive a wedge between you and me. It makes me anxious to imagine you talking to her. We need to talk further about drawing lines around communicating to others about our relationship."

Bill: "I agree. And I can understand your anxiety. I really wasn't clear enough about those lines when she called.

Jeanne: "Thank you. Beyond all this, I need to figure out how to have a calm conversation with my sister, where I let her know how I feel when she talks about me to anyone else but me."

Bill: "Good idea."

Jeanne: "I'm sorry I got so nasty. I really do need to think about my behavior when I get angry."

Bill: "Thanks. I'm no saint either. Actually, I'm glad all this happened. It's an opportunity to talk about things we've been avoiding."

Once the wound starts to close, Jeanne can find her creative energy. When she experiences Bill taking responsibility and continuing to extend empathy toward her, she's able to become a vulnerable partner again and to trust him anew. Consequently, she now begins claiming her own responsibility and can move into examining her own anger.

How to Do This

In order to most effectively show how to get to the bottom of a spat, we're going to resort to a method that we've so far resisted in this book: spelling out a formula. Formulas suggest a cookie-cutter approach—and there is no such thing in emotional intimacy. But there is a definite progression in all spats, a discernible pattern seen here with Bill and Jeanne. In the next chapter, we'll describe four spats that work because they largely follow this pattern.

The Five Elements of a Spat
- Sounding the alarm
- Empathy is experienced (**first turning point**)
- Curiosity trumps fear
- Responsibility is claimed (**second turning point**)
- New emotional depths open up

<u>Element One: Sounding the Alarm</u>

In the spat between Jeanne and Bill, Jeanne sounded a loud, distinct alarm when she arrived at Bill's office trailing a cloud of fury. But in many spats, an inner alarm may ring only faintly, like a small bell in the distance. Still other alarms will register as a sharp prick to one's consciousness, signaling an arrow striking a mark—a stray hurt, a misunderstanding, or an old controversy unearthed.

In every case, though, there will be a certain change in the air between partners. And in the moments following, the most significant decision in the entire spat is then made: whether to voice the alarm. Alternatively, we may minimize feelings, perhaps allow a dark mood to gain entry by practicing some form of evasion, or sink into secret disdain. Any of these moves will invite the peculiar numbness that comes from ignoring and avoiding what needs to be said.

Truth be told, most of us are Olympic medalists at ignoring storm warnings; we also collude with each other in our evasions. To wit: one person sighs with a note of faint exasperation. The other asks, "What's wrong?" The first person says, "Oh, nothing," or deflects the attention to something that isn't at all what's bothering her. The second person is relieved that no alarm has rung after all and gladly lets the matter drop. The original sighing person doesn't press, and the necessary spat gets buried—sure to rattle its bones another day.

If we want to live in a passionately intimate relationship, the loving response to any inner emotional warning we experience ourselves or detect in our partner is to be curious about what it means. Any alarm can prove false, but attentiveness will register nonetheless, increasing a partner's sense of feeling heard. It will also nourish a commitment in the relationship to acknowledge the elephant in the room. This demand for clarity and action won't always make both partners comfortable. It will, however, usher in the fierce satisfactions of real engagement, without which passionate intimacy is hard-pressed to survive.

Element Two: Empathy Is Experienced
(first turning point)

After someone rings an alarm, the next step is to seek clarity about whatever wound has been experienced. Although the best medicine will be the listener's empathy, the picture is clouded by a complexity. Correctly or not, *the listener is also the one perceived to be the source of the wound.*

And right there arises much of the difficulty in pursuing a spat to the bottom. As becomes clear in the spat between Bill and Jeanne, Bill never intended to wound Jeanne by his conversation with her sister. Because it did wound her, though (a reality largely about Jeanne), Bill still had to find his empathy. Nothing else would re-establish the connection between them.

But summoning an empathetic response is not at all straightforward. In a moment of tension and impending conflict, empathy has usually withdrawn behind the barricades. And in its place, an invisible tug-of-war between partners is likely to start, working directly against empathy.

First, defensiveness wants to kick in, and we reach almost automatically for this primitive response. Accused of causing someone pain, we seek cover from such an unflattering self-image. In addition, we are often bedeviled by the mistaken belief that our empathy will be taken for agreement with our partner's point of view. In most cases, though, we don't agree, especially at the outset, and we're straining to hold onto our own perspective—as is our partner, so empathy retreats still further. Juvenile and irrational as this tug-of-war may be, it happens repeatedly because disagreements spike fears (often unconscious) about loss of control and loss of love. And these twin fears block expressions of empathy.

There is an alternative, a sure way to sever the rope in the tug of war. We can choose to stay emotionally open. How? By remembering that:

- we don't need to agree with one another in a heated moment
- we don't need to be defensive

In other words, we can keep our separate opinions and instead of dropping into defensiveness, we can focus attention on what is going on with our wounded partner. We can *consciously decide to attach our attention to empathy*, letting empathy lead the conversation. Later on, we can figure out the events that generated the spat. Right at the moment, the other person is suffering some kind of hurt or fear. And as that person's partner, the most powerful next move is feeling our way into that suffering.

It makes no difference whether the wound someone is experiencing is large, or small, or feels real to us. It's real for that person. And when we, as the listener, can stay with it long enough to hear the shades of meaning, we stop the fruitless tug-of-war. Best of all, it's indisputable that our partner will love us far more for our empathy than for our being "right."

Emotional intimacy is dependent upon each of us keeping our own point of view straight while simultaneously allowing empathy to move toward the other person. Bill and Jeanne's spat demonstrates this. It is Bill's empathy, focused on Jeanne's pain, that enables them to begin to talk about their feelings and behaviors and eventually to acknowledge their blind spots.

Every successful spat tracks this same course to the bottom: each one involves re-experiencing empathy's power. After one partner decides to listen in search of real understanding, empathy can then finally pierce the partner who feels wounded. With empathy building a bridge, we get to the first turning point of the spat; without empathy, we get stuck.

Element Three: Curiosity Trumps Fear

After empathy provides the initial balm during a spat, quieting fears about loss of love and loss of control, then curiosity has room to enter. Creative conversation can begin.

By "curiosity," we don't mean a fact-finding mission to establish what happened; such missions are usually competitive, subtly hostile, and mostly intended to prove who's right. Here's a dead certainty: when we enter the Zone of Being Right, we demonstrate that at least in that moment, we're more intent on power and winning than on love. To recognize this, we only need to recall how defensive or how closed off we become when being right assumes paramount importance for us and locks us into an emotional half nelson.

Once we forego being right or rigidly insisting on who said what to whom, curiosity can gain a foothold. This doesn't mean dropping the empathy. It means tying the empathy to curiosity in order to engage the other person's feelings and perspective. What gets dropped is competition over whose truth is truer.

At that point, a picture like the following begins to take shape, as seen clearly in the encounter between Bill and Jeanne:

- One of us is sufficiently penetrated by a partner's emotional distress to become committed to hearing his feelings. Our empathy allows him to reveal those feelings.
- Becoming genuinely curious and empathetic, we can't fail to be surprised by what we discover about our partner and ourselves.
- During this process we realize that both of our perspectives have value and contain insights that can enrich our relationship.

Curiosity turns out to be simply another form of balm when applied to a spat. If someone trains a full measure of empathetic attention on us, surrenders judgment (almost always born of fear), and is genuinely curious to know how we feel in a particular moment, it's almost impossible not to feel cherished in a startling new way.

We'll grant that this may be rare. Our attention gets easily deflected; impatience drives us to move on in a hurry. Whatever the reason for turning away from each other, in doing so, we leave a wake of loneliness. We're not suggesting that a partner's curiosity will cure all loneliness in a relationship. But when curiosity is real and strong, it cuts loneliness down to size.

<u>Element Four: Responsibility Is Claimed</u>
(second turning point)

Beyond every "I'm sorry," beyond our empathizing and curiosity, stands the necessity to claim responsibility for whatever we've each contributed, knowingly or not, to a particular situation.

On the way to the bottom of every spat, a signature moment arrives when both of us have to belly up to the emotional bar and slap down our personal cash on the barrelhead of responsibility. This responsibility falls into three closely related categories; all three have to be in place for both partners to feel they've reached the bottom.

To begin with, each partner needs to take responsibility for identifying his or her own feelings and be willing to communicate them. That may seem elementary, but it isn't. Many of us avoid this—we shy away from talking about our feelings or say we don't know what we feel. In an emotionally passionate relationship, however, we can't passively seek refuge in such "not knowing"; we have to take active responsibility for figuring out our feelings.

When we don't do this, we send a surplus of unclear messages that require endless mind reading by our partner. Furthermore, when we don't engage what we're really feeling and articulate it, hidden agendas of all sorts start asserting their undermining power. Anger, hurt, and fear inevitably become dominant strains in the relationship. This shadow boxing with phantoms will stop, however, when we consistently take responsibility for what we feel, at the time we feel it, and voice it clearly. Not voicing our feelings reduces us, ultimately, to a kind of infantalization. It's no coincidence that the origin of the word "infant" means "incapable of speech."

Next, we each need to claim responsibility for our own behavior, for what we do with our feelings. This is a confusing and contrary idea, since in a hot moment, many of us will leap quickly into blaming others for *causing* our behavior, holding them responsible for our words or actions. For example:

> She says, "I wouldn't have been so nasty
> to you if you hadn't yelled at me!"

We imagine that our partner "started" the trouble between us, and we're therefore justified in responding with matching ugliness. But justification isn't the issue. No matter how tempting it is to think otherwise, our words and behaviors are our own, and we are responsible for them.

This is hard to swallow; it *seems* as though we wouldn't have been nasty without being provoked. It doesn't feel like a choice . . . we're nobler than that and wouldn't have said something rotten unless pushed into it! But the truth lies elsewhere. If we throw down a nasty comment in response to being yelled at, then the nastiness is on us, not on our partner for provoking us. We make choices about being defensive and reactive, and we don't get to blame anyone else for those choices.

Finally, each of us has to be responsible for our own blind spots. This begins with acknowledging that we have blind spots in the first place—a prospect many of us could cheerfully skip. A short list of blind spots makes it plain why we'd rather not own up: inability to hear that we are too harsh (or too easy) on children; assuming our partner can run the family house mostly solo; overlooking the effect on our family life if we spend most of our time at work; ignoring how our impatience sounds to other people; repeatedly forgetting a partner's request to put the toilet seat down . . . and so forth.

Blind spots cause chaos in day-to-day living. If one person has a blind spot, for instance, about arriving late for dates or plans and is constantly sliding into place at the last minute with breathless apology, there's really only one cure: do something new. This doesn't suggest psychotherapy. Taking responsibility for a blind spot is about acknowledging some behavior that's weakening a relationship, and then not just winking at it yet another time but stopping it.

It's common for a spat to get stuck at this last point of taking responsibility. In building a bridge between us, we may manage to locate some empathy and summon curiosity but then fail to take responsibility and actually do things differently. The refrain is an old one:

"We've talked about this over and over!"

We sure have. It's as though we arrive at the last six inches of the bridge and retreat, rather than go forward to make real change. In effect, the second turning point of the spat eludes us, and once again, we get stuck. Living in a passionately intimate relationship demands deep willingness to see creative change through to the end. It involves moving away from willful chaos in the relationship, becoming partners that recognize where change has to happen, and trying to respond with speed and grace.

Ultimately, taking responsibility in all these ways will not only herald the bottom of a spat but will also lead naturally into re-establishing goodwill. After all, when we're both shouldering our share of the responsibility, then we can both rightfully expect to receive a share of the mercy.

There's one last note to be struck here about a type of sabotage that will short-circuit taking responsibility, effectively barring the path to the bottom of a spat. This sabotage involves emotionally rescuing a partner. We tell ourselves that continuing to pursue the truth of a particular issue will "hurt him," and so we back off, supposedly in an attempt to shield him.

We need to acknowledge, in these instances, that we are actually shielding ourselves. Realizing that the consequence of pursuing the truth will be threatening or painful for *us*, we stop short to protect ourselves. And the consequence is some version of a false bottom—forgiving too quickly, agreeing to disagree, settling for a phony resolution, accepting compromises that are bound to unravel. No matter what, rescuing ourselves (or each other) from telling the whole truth inevitably means failing to clean out the wound and missing the real bottom in the bargain.

<u>Element Five: New Emotional Depths Open Up</u>

Every spat taken to the bottom shifts the ground of a relationship, even if only slightly. Spats jolt us awake. Every place of tension holds an opportunity to see behind the masks we each wear, interrupting the routine of daily life. Necessary though that routine is, we don't actually learn much about our partner or see one another fully, when we're clacking comfortably along the tracks of the status quo. Frequently, we need to smack into an obstacle before we will sit up and pay attention. And those obstacles turn out to be containers that, when opened, spill out much gold about our inner lives. They reveal what we yearn for, what hurts us, what causes us to be lonely, and what makes us feel loved.

Spats fully finished take us down into the deeper layers of the relationship. We get to experience each other anew and, if we're lucky, we find out that we didn't know as much about our partner as we thought we did. If we opt for mere compromise, though, when ending a spat, not much revelation is likely to occur. Compromise is about problem solving, not about intimacy. Compromises tend to halt revelations about ourselves, leaving us largely hidden behind our masks. Spats followed to a truly satisfying ending, however, bring us into an emerging new understanding, inviting us out into the sunshine, rendering us much more transparent and knowable.

A spat rightly engaged, all the way down to the bottom, may not feel so good while we're doing it, but if we'll join hands and stick with it, we will eventually emerge onto higher, broader ground.

This is just what happened with Bill and Jeanne. At the end of the spat, Jeanne was able to imagine a new way of talking with Bill about her anger, and they had tackled hard questions about the boundaries between their personal and private lives. Other issues may await exploration—like whether it was okay for Jeanne to come bursting into Bill's office in the first place, and whether Bill has a tendency to divulge too much information about their relationship. No matter what issues remain, though, the point holds. The true bottom of any spat will be shot through with emotional intimacy, born out of facing our conflicts squarely.

"The story of human intimacy is one of constantly allowing ourselves to see those we love most deeply in a new, more fractured, light. Look hard. Risk that."

Cheryl Strayed

CHAPTER 10

Four Resolved Spats

The Five Elements of a Spat set out in the last chapter now need additional illustrations showing how to apply them. The examples given here are all drawn from real-life situations, adapted to show how to reach the turning points we've described.

One clarifying note: if the spats feel stagy, it's because this is a teaching tool. Language in this context invariably sounds contrived when compared to actual talk. The people in these examples, though, are being intentionally pictured as working their way through the Five Elements. Employing everyday dilemmas, each spat shows how to come to the heart of the issue fast, uses words that will work in moments of tension, continues to press toward the bottom, and generates a minimum amount of heat.

These spats also focus on wounds that might appear small but aren't. And each one suggests that while we may be sorely tempted to get embroiled in the subject matter of a spat, it's a sure-fire way to get lost. The wound is the entry point; the feelings coming from that wound are what need to be heard. And empathetic listening is the only effective initial response—over and over again.

Chloe and Jim Skirmish Over an Old Issue: Control

If we're listening to ourselves, we have to admit that all of us can occasionally be drawn into power struggles with a partner. These may occur over seemingly minor subjects, but they can turn into a major problem in many relationships. In this instance, Jim and Chloe are in the kitchen, where she is mixing up what appears to him to be a very large batch of food for the dog.

Jim: "You're not going to give her all *that*, are you?"

Chloe: (speaking to the dog in a mocking voice) "Your father doesn't want you to have this."

Jim: (peeved) "I didn't say that."

Ten minutes later, Jim approaches Chloe and tentatively sounds an alarm (Element One).

Jim: "I don't understand what just happened."

Chloe: "I felt stung by you."

Jim: "You sounded so sarcastic."

Chloe: "I did?"

Jim: "It felt like it to me."

Chloe: "Well, I didn't mean to be sarcastic. I realize now that I was aggravated with you for intruding yourself into my feeding the dog. I felt insulted when you implied I didn't know any better than to give her three days' worth of food at once."

Chloe is surprised by an old blind spot (sarcasm) reappearing and takes immediate responsibility for returning to respectful talk. Her quick and specific identification of why Jim's comment insulted her brings clarity to the spat.

Jim: "I guess I hurt your feelings."

Reaching for empathy (Element Two), Jim names the primary feeling Chloe is likely experiencing but not stating. Once Chloe hears his empathy she slips into the pocket of safety it creates, and then can acknowledge that Jim is correct.

Chloe: "Yes, you did."

Jim: "I'm very sorry."

Chloe: "Thank you."

The **first turning point in the spat** occurs when Jim's empathy finds its mark. Curiosity (Element Three) can now enter the conversation.

141

Chloe: "Jim, it seems to me this happens a lot in our relationship. I often feel controlled by you."

Jim: "What do you mean?"

Chloe: "If I told you how frustrating it is that you seem to comment on everything I do, I think my sarcasm might pop out less often."

Jim: "I'm just trying to help."

Chloe: "Maybe so, but can you hear why that feels intrusive?"

Jim: "Yes."

Chloe: "Do you suppose there's more to this?"

Chloe gently confronts Jim about a touchy issue—her experience of his controlling behavior. Her artful questions invite his continuing empathy and reflection.

Jim: "Of course, I have to acknowledge that it isn't the first time I've heard about this from you. And coworkers have spoken to me about it. I can see why it feels intrusive, and I'm sorry."

The **second turning point in the spat** is reached. Jim is starting to take responsibility (Element Four) for his behavior, even though the blind spot about his being controlling remains mostly in place.

Chloe: "Jim, thank you. I want you to know that it's easiest to forgive you when you'll talk to me about this."

Jim: "Well, I'll try."

Chloe introduces forgiveness into the conversation, signaling her desire for closeness and what will promote it. From here on out, new depths (Element Five) open up.

Chloe: "I don't like feeling estranged. I'd love to explore ways to understand how we can be closer. The next time you sense you're about to be intrusive, maybe you could tell me how you're feeling before you speak."

Jim: "That sounds hard."

Chloe: "It probably is hard. I believe we're never going to be really happy together, though, until we both get more aware of how we affect each other."

By using her personal authority, Chloe challenges Jim to look at what might bring them more contentment.

Jim: "All of this makes me think I'm like my dad."

Chloe stays quiet and attentive.

Jim: "You know, in some ways it's a relief to actually think and talk about what drives me to do what I do."

Chloe: "When you talk to me about your feelings, I feel much closer to you."

Jim: "It's hard. My family never talked about feelings, and I'm not so good at it either."

Chloe: "Well, I've got some of the same problem. Where do you think I learned to be sarcastic? My mother was an ace at sarcasm, and my parents lived in a constant near-battlefield state. I don't want that for myself or for you."

Jim: "I don't either."

Chloe: "You have no idea how much—instead of biting you—I want to understand you better and be understood by you. I know my sarcasm is hurtful. I really need to learn how to do things differently."

Jim: "Thanks. Obviously, me too."

Jim and Chloe have rendered themselves quite vulnerable and as a result have arrived at a place where tension can resolve into affection. The anxiety raised in this kitchen spat is not only gone, but the desire to "win" the power struggle has been trumped by gaining insight into one another. Emotional doors are opening; intimacy is replacing estrangement.

Sam and Becky Handle a Hard Public Moment

The issue here is dealing with a relationship's public face versus its private one. How do we remain ourselves in a group setting and stay intimately related to our partner? At a small dinner party, Becky said publicly to her husband, Sam, "You're getting loud." Sam had enough detachment to choose not to respond at the dinner table. On the way home, with silence filling the car, Becky attempted to open a conversation.

Becky: "You're kind of quiet."

Sam: "I'm not happy with you."

Becky: "Well, you were embarrassing me."

Becky has spoken up (Element One) and quickly confirmed why the air seems poisoned.

Sam: "I was the embarrassed one. You publicly reprimanded me."

Sam stands his ground. This kind of reprimand has happened before, and they've agreed that it's off limits in their relationship.

Becky: "I can see why you were embarrassed. I would have been hurt if you had done that to me."

Sam: "Thank you."

The **first turning point** arises out of Becky's swift and effective empathizing (Element Two), without resorting to defensiveness. Now there is room for curiosity (Element Three) about what was going on below the surface.

Sam: "What happened to you back at the table?"

Becky: I got nervous when the voices seemed to get louder. I don't like strenuous debates, as you know."

Sam: "I do know. That behavior usually reminds you of your mother's alcoholic rants."

Becky: "Yes, it does."

Sam: "Do you think my behavior was anything like hers?"

Becky: "No, but you guys *were* getting loud."

Sam: (silent for a minute) "I'm wondering if you would be willing to find a way to figure out whether a public situation is truly out of control, or if it's more about your own anxiety that it *will* get out of control."

Becky: "Yes. That's fair . . . sure."

The **second turning point** comes from Becky's openness to accepting responsibility (Element Four) for her anxiety in this situation. She knows that when her fear is spiked, she has to get better at being detached and exercising her own authority. They now enter some deeper, more vulnerable territory (Element Five).

Becky: "I feel pretty dumb."

Sam: "I'm sorry about that. I don't want you to feel dumb. We all get anxious and blurt stuff out."

Becky: "I suppose, but I feel like sort of a slow learner."

Sam: "Maybe it would help if we got some signals between us to use in public so we could navigate moments like these better."

Becky: "That's a good idea."

Sam: "I'm sorry the situation made you anxious."

Becky: "I wish I hadn't embarrassed you. Are you still angry?"

Sam: "No—really, I'm not. I forgive you."

Becky: "Thanks. That makes me happy."

As Becky and Sam begin to look at how to be more creative, more united, in public situations, it's clear that there's now a bridge between them. Becky ends the spat by checking to be sure Sam's anger has abated. She is able to feel new confidence after sensing that the spat is truly resolved and hearing she's forgiven.

Steve and Jennifer Grapple with Their Blended Family

Jennifer and Steve are in a second marriage. They each have adult children from their previous marriages and are continuing the work of creating a blended family. Not surprisingly, their most severe challenge lies in issues about each other's children. Following yet another incident of tension between Jennifer, and Steve's daughter Susan, Jennifer launches into a conversation.

Jen: "Steve, Susan is a real problem. I babysit for her for free, and I never get a word of thanks. She's spoiled and irresponsible—and worse, you defend her!"

Jen has definitively invoked Element One.
Steve remains quiet.

Jen: "And you never do anything about it."

Steve: "I don't know what to do."

Jen: "You always take her side."

Steve: "I do not . . . and this isn't getting us anywhere."

Four hours pass before beginning again. Steve is determined not to be drawn into an argument about the facts, as Jen was previously doing, but instead to try to focus on feelings.

Jen: "Do you want to talk?"

Steve: "I'm really not sure what to say. I just feel so sad."

Jen: "And I feel mad."

Steve: "Yes, I understand that you're angry and have *been* angry about this."

Once she experiences Steve's acknowledgment that she's angry, Jen is drawn into exploring his feelings.

Jen: "Tell me more about why you feel sad."

Steve: "Because the two people I love most don't get along."

Jen: "Well, I've tried everything with her."

Steve: "Wait a minute . . . I'm not suggesting it's your fault. The whole thing just makes me incredibly sad."

Jen: "Well, it does me too."

Steve: "Yes, I believe that. You try so hard."

Jen: "Thank you for saying so. Sometimes I get scared that you blame me."

Steve: "I'm sorry. I really don't mean to sound blaming."

Jen: "Thanks."

First Turning Point. Steve's insistent focus on feelings leads them eventually into mutual empathizing (Element Two) about how hurt and anxious everyone is in this situation. As anxiety diminishes, curiosity finds room.

Steve: "How did we get into this mess?"

With these words of inquiry (Element Three), Steve sounds a note of kinship and invitation to look together at what now feels more like a common problem.

Jen: "Well, I know I'm not always easy to live with and can be demanding."

Steve: "We've all contributed to the difficulty we're having—Susan, too. I know many of the things you say about her are true."

Jen: "I don't remember you ever saying that."

Steve: "Because I hate conflict. *(Steve is quiet for a moment.)* We could work on this together, you know."

Jen: "How?"

Steve: "I could try to speak up more, and you could tell me sooner what's bothering you."

Jen: "It's helpful for you to suggest we could both do something new. I know if I hold my feelings in it causes trouble. It feels good to me when you admit that what you do also feeds the fire."

Steve: "It doesn't help that I get nervous when conflict arises and then shut down."

Second Turning Point. Together, Steve and Jen are able to admit the situation has two sides—three, counting Susan's. When both of them take responsibility (Element Four) for themselves, their new sense of connection allows for expanded ways of relating to each other (Element Five).

Jen: "When you shut down, it scares me. Getting mad at you feels better than being powerless to get you to talk."

Steve: "I know I need to stay in the conversation."

Jen: "Maybe if I lowered the volume and changed my tone, you'd listen more to how I experience Susan."

Steve: "I would. Whenever I hear you express any affection, even if you're frustrated with her, it's easy to trust you. I know you care about her."

Jen: "I do. And I also get anxious about how to handle my relationship with her."

Steve: "And I get caught between you, not knowing what to do."

Jen: "Maybe we can start over. Now that we at least are more aware of how we both feel, maybe we can figure out some ways to splice this family together that will work for everyone."

Steve: "I do like the kind of conversation we're having now. I've got many things I'd really like to talk about with you. Besides, all this tension over Susan has been ruining our sex life."

Jen: "Yes, it has. I don't want to make love with somebody I'm mad at or who shuts himself off from me."

Steve: "Let's keep talking. I miss you."

Jen: "I miss you too."

Jen and Steve are starting to create a safer emotional relationship. By the end, each has revealed some blind spots, stayed focused on feelings, and kept empathetically listening to the other. Anxiety is replaced by curiosity, and it's clearer that both anger and affection play a role in being close. If they can maintain the current tenor, it will be much easier to approach the difficult issues about Susan non-judgmentally. The possibility of forging a stronger and more stable blended family has come distinctly into view.

David and Tom Remove a Thorn

We suggested earlier that spats will occur—or need to occur—between close friends and family members, as well as between intimate partners. David and Tom are old friends who have been buying each other breakfast roughly once a week for over a decade. The conversation begins with warm greetings and small talk. Fairly quickly, however, Tom says he wants to talk about something. This spat is included, in part, to show that the Five Elements don't always occur in sequence.

Tom: "David, I need to talk about something that happened at our last breakfast."

David: "Okay."

Tom: "It was painful for me last week, when—"

David: (interrupting) "Oh, I know what you're going to say."

Tom: (pausing) "It was painful when you said that I usually order a more expensive breakfast when it's your week to buy."

Tom has sounded the alarm (Element One), been brief, and now waits, hoping David is willing to empathize with how he felt.
David remains quiet.

Tom: "I felt embarrassed."

David: (after further silence) "I sometimes make off-hand remarks."

Tom continues to wait without speaking, giving David some room, hoping that he won't minimize the feelings he's expressed.

David: "And I do believe off-hand remarks come from somewhere. This doesn't reflect well on me. *(long pause)* I do find myself slightly annoyed sometimes, not about this, but remember that we get together for breakfast because that meets your needs in regard to work. I would choose lunch or dinner. At times, I sense a lingering resentment in me about this."

David is revealing himself and what might account for his behavior. He's not defensive. Instead, he's being transparent, so Tom can see his motivation.

David: "However, I reject the idea that off-hand comments are 'about nothing.' And in fact, I'm well aware that when we can't remember whose week it is to pay, you always grab the check. Sorry for my words."

The First and Second Turning Points are reached simultaneously. David's willingness to immediately claim responsibility (Element Four), along with taking Tom's feelings seriously, combine into effective empathy (Element Two). In addition, he has apologized.

Tom: "Thank you. I'm relieved."

David: "Very sorry it happened."

This spat could be considered resolved. Tom presses on, though, into curiosity (Element Three) about what might lie below the surface.

Tom: "Let's take this further. After thinking over your original comment about my ordering more expensively—and judging you harshly, something I regret—I stopped and asked myself whether you see something about me that I don't see."

David: "No, I don't think so."

Curious about his own blind spots, Tom invites an opportunity for learning more about himself and for the two of them to continue to know each other better. In other words, he deliberately opens the path to Element Five.

Tom: "Well, maybe not. But it did occur to me that I *might* order more inexpensively for myself on days that I'm paying and feeling short of cash. However, I want you to know that I think of you as my guest on those mornings and want *you* to order whatever you like. In reverse, I think I do consider myself as your guest and order what I want when you are picking up the tab."

David: "Of course. That makes sense."

By exploring this encounter further, David and Tom have figured out why David, at first, might have thought Tom was taking advantage of him. The thorn is extracted; they are at the bottom of the spat.

Tom: "Well, I say all this because I want you to understand how I experience myself and also get clear for the future. I really appreciate your openness. Are we done with this?"

David: "I think so. Are you?"

Tom: "Yes. Your responses feel very genuine to me."

By sharing their feelings and making their motivations transparent, David and Tom have not only extracted the thorn but have further enriched their relationship.

David: "You know, I'm really happy we had this conversation."

Tom: "Me too. I don't want to carry resentments around. You're too important to me."

A certain lightheartedness has entered the conversation. Real resolution of a persisting tension usually produces relief, satisfaction, and increased good humor.

In these four examples, we don't want to imply that spats will carry us to some heavenly realm where anger dissolves, blind spots vanish, 20/20 vision reigns, and spats themselves disappear—quite the opposite. In a passionate life, *because we are alive to our feelings as they unfold,* spats will keep occurring. Our job is to engage them with spirit and growing confidence that we can at least put the issues raised down for a solid nap, if not grant them permanent sleep.

Be sure, however, that if people resembling Jim and Chloe remain alive to themselves and to each other, they will tangle anew over feelings of being controlled; Becky and Sam will experience again the injury of a public trespass; Jennifer and Steve will still lose their grip over the complexity of relating to each other's children; and Tom and David will get pierced again by misunderstanding. In every case, this will happen as long as partners and friends and family members continue to care for each other and are willing to press forward toward some new vulnerable depth of feeling in the relationship. The choice, ultimately, comes down to that: depths or shallows. The fortunate among us end up in the depths.

"I could drink a case of you and still be standing."

Joni Mitchell

CHAPTER 11

Living Along the Passionate Edge

At this point, the canny reader will ask, does all this hard work add up? Is it worth the effort required to alter our attitudes and perspectives, to learn and practice the kinds of skills essential for emotional intimacy? Obviously, our response is a strong yes. Any relationship that embraces the suggestions given in these pages will—with infinite variation—reap a variety of rich rewards.

We have said that joy, not simply happiness, is the point of a passionate relationship. Not the "joy" associated with unrelenting cheerfulness but the joy that comes from keenly experiencing being loved, and being invited to love freely in return. We have used the word love in this book infrequently, and yet it has, of course, been the ground of everything said. The rewards set out at this point are all about deep knowing and loving . . . in a life that brings sustained joy and distinct exhilaration.

Energy Goes Way Up

By now it is surely evident that in ongoing relationships where tension is overlooked and disagreements are ignored, energy will drop. Engagement with one another can eventually begin to feel like too much trouble; it may even start to seem like a hopeless proposition. Eyeball rolling and muttered sighs become the order of the day, and comments like, "We're just so different," serve as justification for evading difficult issues. The issues themselves may not be large, but the energy required to settle them feels huge. Eventually, the emotional wires that once carried the current in the relationship don't have enough voltage to stay taut, and they sag under their own weight.

On the other hand, when necessary spats do occur, energy can get restored like lost electrical power to a line. The way we deal with anger proves the point. If we voice our anger and it gets heard, it has a chance to dissipate—often quickly. If we swallow it, it goes into the invisible but very real sack on our back, joining all the other leftover anger we've been stashing in that sack. And with every new piece of anger added, it takes more energy to haul the sack around.

How much better it is to grapple with whatever is happening to us, even if what's happening makes us anxious. When we voice the emotion we're experiencing right here, right now, we not only stop wasting energy holding that emotion in, but we usually experience a lift, a surge of new energy. It's as though a switch is thrown, and our sagging emotional wires are snapped straight again.

Spontaneity Gets a New Lease

When we let the passionate edge in our lives get blunted, it often means we're tolerating a lot of cautious hesitation. We're picking our way through emotional minefields, dispatching border patrols around potentially explosive subjects. Under such guard, spontaneity is usually the first casualty.

One of the chief rewards of claiming, or reclaiming, a passionate intimacy with our partner is the new life breathed into the spontaneity between us. When we no longer measure our words for fear of setting off a bomb, because we now trust that bombs can be successfully defused, a new spontaneity can emerge. And with it comes a fresh sense of freedom. Freedom to play, to have fun, to laugh at ourselves and one another, and to take emotional risks again that we may have long ago stopped taking.

Furthermore, and most crucially, this process of restoring spontaneity is cumulative. If partners learn to have creative spats, going to the bottom of the barrel, and completely vanquishing whatever demon has reared its head, layers of trust get built on top of one another. We begin to see that most issues truly *can* get resolved. Assumptions, expectations, and even values can frequently be worked through and agreed upon, to the point of creating a more durable bond. The result is that we start to feel known by our partner in a far fuller sense. We calm down internally, we lower our defenses, we stop hedging our emotional bets. In a word, our trust grows and then becomes the source of continuing spontaneity.

We Can Stop Hiding

Passionate engagement with a partner usually brings an end to our multiple ways of emotionally hiding from one another—by which we mean covering up our feelings, pretending to feelings we don't have, putting on false faces, and going along with things we really don't want to do. Quitting hiding, moreover, decreases the amount of loneliness we feel. Whether our loneliness is subtle or overt, pervasive or fleeting, it's fed by hiding; it subsides as we are able to risk showing more and more of our true face.

Giving up hiding is also exactly what happens in a creative spat, since we can't resolve a spat and remain emotionally invisible. By definition, we have to let ourselves be seen. But that can be a scary prospect. What if we reveal our hearts and get rejected, or judged, or stared at blankly? Fears like these can sabotage our impulse to reveal much of anything, trapping us into settling for a measure of loneliness. Better to stay hidden and a bit lonely than to be exposed and vulnerable . . . or so we imagine.

Conquering such fears leads to powerful rewards. When the spat becomes a trusted opportunity instead of a clash to be avoided, any win/lose mode of relating (and its associated loneliness) gets left in the dust—where it belongs. If tension and conflict are sidestepped, we end up living in separate rooms of our emotional house, and loneliness prospers. But if two people create the safety to reveal themselves more completely, then every spat can be aimed at a mutual win: empathetic understanding, a lightening of spirits, and a palpable lessening of loneliness.

In addition, when we stop hiding we gain access to a wide expanse of virgin territory in the relationship. Many of us have watched couples in restaurants eat in near-total silence, anxiously wondering whether we're staring at our own future . . . as though there's a finite amount of "material" between us that will eventually dry up. That worry becomes meaningless when we come out of hiding. We are unlikely to find ourselves with nothing to talk about when we can talk freely about what we're feeling and know that we'll get heard. If we experience an enlarged freedom to be ourselves, then our selves keep on growing and always have something to say. This of course spells the death of "how-was-your-day-oh-fine," when it isn't the truth. That kind of superficiality gets elbowed out of a life passionately lived for the simple reason that it isn't very interesting.

Finally, ending our hiding also means not being on the run from *ourselves* any more. Often the loneliness we experience isn't caused by hiding from someone else but from ourselves—not admitting what we really feel, or need, or want. Think sexual issues. Some of the greatest difficulty in our sexual relationships stems from hesitancy about acknowledging our desires and articulating our anxieties. Yet when we call a halt to hiding and let ourselves be known and loved in new ways, we will experience an exhilaration that's layered with energy, relief, gratitude, and openness.

In any community, and certainly in a community of two, thriving depends on continuing to become more and more our true selves, ever clearer about who we are. But that clarity becomes possible only to whatever extent we come out of hiding. In the end, a great relationship insists we take the emotional risks involved in claiming our own authority, finding our own voice, and sharing these with our partner. Think of people who seem to manifest the most passion and vitality in their lives. Aren't they also the ones able to show their deepest feelings, bravely say what they think, and live out loud instead of in hiding?

Another Kind of Nakedness Emerges

Mary illustrates this nakedness in a story about a visit to a family graveyard:

"At the foot of Mt. Equinox, in Manchester, Vermont, there's a beautiful old cemetery containing Tom's family graves—some as ancient as the early 1800s; others as recent as his own parents and brother.

"Every autumn, when the Vermont hills blaze crimson and gold, we come back to this cemetery carrying buckets of chrysanthemums, clippers to trim old lilac bushes, and armloads of poignant memories.

"On our most recent visit, we were eager to see the names we'd arranged to be engraved on one of the stones—a cherished elderly aunt and a cousin of Tom's who'd died too young, with whom he'd always summered as a child, both to be etched into the same piece of granite as Tom's grandparents.

"At one point, as the waning afternoon sun turned the whole graveyard luminous rose, I found Tom bent down in front of this most recent engraving. I saw him tracing the names on the stone with his finger. He was crying softly. Although this clearly began as a private moment, he didn't stop when he realized I was standing near him. Slowly, deliberately, he kept moving his fingers over each letter, nakedly present, again, to these recent losses, and now present to me."

This kind of vulnerable encounter comes from living along the passionate edge. Its "nakedness" is really about the willingness to enter regions of raw emotion, allowing our complicated humanity to be seen. We're not suggesting an intrusive "peering into" or sharing every detail of our innermost thoughts; those are intolerable ideas. Indeed, a drive to know someone completely is demonic.

But there *is* a type of knowing that reaches into a realm of deep intimacy, into a place of compassion and communion. There might be conversation in this realm, but there isn't likely to be much chat. At least not the anxious, filling-the-air chat that all of us can resort to from time to time because real presence to strong emotion makes us nervous.

Experiences like this one—of resonant seeing and knowing our partner—will often lead to profound depth in a relationship. And in turn, this deep knowing feeds the mystery of enduring attraction. That includes enduring sexual attraction. It's worth noting that, in the biblical tradition, the Hebrew word for "knowing," in the sexual sense, can't be separated from emotional connection. Knowing a person sexually involved knowing his or her emotional nakedness. In our own time, tending as we do to associate nakedness primarily with sex, this much richer understanding of nakedness easily gets lost.

A similar loss occurs in the way we use the word *erotic*. It has come to be synonymous with sex, especially with sexual titillation. But the Greek word *Eros*, from which we derive erotic, is actually about desire for meaningful connection that will overcome separateness. What we yearn for is not simply the joining of body parts but the emotional joining of selves, which is what we receive when we know one another far beyond the surfaces. To say we are "making love" to someone we do not know is a contradiction in terms.

We Experience Healing, Wholeness, a Larger Life

A primary payoff of living on the passionate edge is that life gets larger. This is chiefly a result of learning emotional lessons from one another—once we are open enough to let that happen. Our own life together offers a case in point:

> "When we came into this relationship, Mary was convinced that an angry exchange between us was going to end up making her feel bad about herself. She thought anger was tied to punishment—not actual but emotional. It took some time before she really believed that my anger was simply me, expressing a feeling, not my wanting to 'punish' her."

> "Once upon a time, Tom thought that if I gave him a strong, articulate response to something, I was trying to control him. I just wanted to be taken seriously and was willing to be strenuous about it. Of course, I'm not above having moments of being controlling. I needed him to understand, though, that control wasn't the point for me; engagement with him was."

This boils down to letting ourselves be inspired by a partner—literally, letting that person breathe new life into stale, airless places—and absorbing how he or she models another way of doing things. It hinges on our willingness to let our guard down far enough and long enough to admit to being flawed, allowing ourselves to be a student, a beginner. It goes back to the earlier discussion of blind spots: if we can let them be seen and finally loved away, we become more whole and our lives get correspondingly larger.

When the kind of learning we're describing here takes place, it means that empathy and curiosity have finally gotten married—no minor match. Given how hard it is to summon either of these capacities, summoning both and joining them ushers in wholeness and healing. Take again the example of anger. It's only when we can admit we don't know how to deal with anger, acknowledge we need empathy for how poorly we *are* dealing with it, and become curious about how to do it differently that we have the remotest chance of learning anything new. However, when this openness about doing something new does occur, it has the power to be transformational. If, over time, we learn to bring life and light to what was formerly dark and tight, our spirits eventually open wider, and an emotional part of ourselves gradually gets transformed from smaller to larger.

Once we approach each other with empathy and curiosity, then the power struggle that can infect every relationship (in guises both obvious and obscure) will stop. Here's the sure bet: if we don't feel loved, we'll reach for control. But if we feel cared about, listened to, and included, then the need for control abates. A shorthand way of understanding this is to see that we can have power or we can have love—we can't have both. We don't mean that partners surrender their own personal power in a relationship. But when each partner surrenders the *drive* for power and control (which often translates as the desire to be right, to win), then love and vulnerability will get revealed as the far greater prizes.

Once we surrender a my-way-or-the-highway perspective, we become more interested in what we can "birth" together, in creative collaboration. Consider the seemingly mundane example of putting together a home. If one person has ironclad, rigid ideas about how a home should look, with only grudging room for a partner's desires, birthing a new home together will not happen. The test for whether we've birthed anything new is easy: does whatever we've created encourage us to thrive as individuals *and* as partners? If so, then the best self in each of us has been given new life.

A Deeper Intimacy

Embracing a life of emotional depth is the point of this book, and yet how difficult it is to do. Life wounds us, again and again, in the blink of an eye, wiping out even the dim awareness that we've closed ourselves off . . . until something kick-starts our consciousness, and we return to being present again.

Reaping the rewards of deeper intimacy requires, above all, that we continue to plumb the emotional depths of the relationship and take the risk of living into the truth we find there. That can often be complicated, as Tom illustrates in the following story:

"At one point in our lives, Mary and I lived in New York City and were working in a job with lots of pressure and stress.

Eventually, this expressed itself in our sexual relationship. Perplexed about what was happening, we had a conversation that drew us tightly together.

"On the afternoon of that conversation, we went out to buy groceries. Striding along Third Avenue, arm in arm, Mary suddenly took a giant step forward, turned, and looked fiercely and lovingly into my face. 'I want you to know something,' she said, 'I'm staying with you for the rest of my life, even if you never have another erection.'

"I stopped dead in my tracks. Can my wife actually be saying this to me while traffic flies by and taxis blare? Ten percent of me felt an internal eruption of fear and pain, but 90 percent of me was astonished by her bold declaration. Would she stay, regardless? Maybe not. Some anxious part of us is never quite sure what might be a deal breaker. But there was no question about one thing: I now knew myself loved with a generosity and depth way beyond what I had previously understood or absorbed.

"I stood there, amazed by her behavior. And then, our walk down Third Avenue continued as though it was a normal grocery outing. I heard no more from her. She didn't try to fix me, or rescue me, or even be supportive in any further way. She had spoken her heart and trusted I would work it out for myself. And, no surprise, our sexual challenges immediately began to disappear."

Coming Home

Amazement. Surprise. Aliveness. Enthusiasm. Joy. And more than a little anxiety. These are the signposts marking the road along the passionate edge, the indicators telling us that the road is the right one, pointing us toward home. And "home" isn't just a metaphor to fling out here at the end of the book. It's where we've been headed from the start and is the reason why we might bother to embark on this quest in the first place: we all yearn for an emotional home and long to find it at the center of our primary relationships.

For many of us, home might be defined as a place to be emotionally real, where we can acknowledge our fully flawed selves and lay down the exhausting burden of wearing a mask. But home is elusive. Our original families, for example, can frequently disappoint us on this score; when we go home to them, we may be *least* likely to let our hair down. This is especially true if families tend to dismiss our enthusiasms or meet them with exaggerated support that doesn't feel genuine.

When we experience either of these responses or some subtle variation, we end up feeling misunderstood. At the least, we don't feel satisfyingly engaged. Acknowledging this, however, sometimes just creates new difficulties—hurt feelings, or silences, and an amplified sense of being misunderstood. So we keep the truest part of ourselves under wraps and endure a certain alienation and loneliness. This doesn't mean many of us don't also leap with joy at the prospect of "going home." It's just that we are likely to park our fully alive selves at the threshold, wishing the sign over the door to the family home would say *engagement* but knowing that it often doesn't.

That's one reason why we come to crave deep emotional engagement with a partner. We yearn for the at-home-ness of being known and cherished anyway; of having someone encourage our enthusiasms and support us in setting those enthusiasms loose. We want a companion on the journey . . . literally, a bread-sharer who breaks life open with us and for us, relishing every last morsel until we've both eaten our fill.

That is, finally, the prize that living on the passionate edge delivers: the deep peace of coming home to ourselves and being instrumental in the process of our partner doing likewise. Rarely is the dance a smooth tango at the start. But as our best selves come forward, prompting us to fully extend our arms to one another, we find we can embrace the dance we've always wanted. And as we glide at last into a high-spirited tango, we can say, with equal strength of feeling: I utterly adore you, *and* you drive me nuts, and let me tell you why both are true.

ACKNOWLEDGMENTS

Many thanks to our editor, Jennifer Nolan, for the graceful way she held our feet to the fire, lending her artful spirit to shaping this book. Likewise to our initial editors, Sascha Alper and Larry Weissman, for helping us bring the book into focus many months ago.

We also want to thank a flock of faithful readers for tackling sections of the book-in-process: Marie and Dave Dittmer, Laurie Fisher, Nina Frost and Robert Close, Peggy Keyser, Amey Leadley, Melinda Meisner, and Kate Wilkinson and Peter Stoops. And for the great technical help we've been given, we take our hats off to Ariette Scott—as well as to Robin Cushman Phillips and Althea Dugliss.

To Sharon and Bill Schambra for their invaluable support from the very beginning to the end; to our longtime friend and writer companion, Kate Kennedy, for all her loving encouragement; and to David Sanford, for his unflagging enthusiasm and curiosity—to each of you we extend our abiding gratitude.

ABOUT THE AUTHORS

Following their graduation from Yale Divinity School, Mary and Tom were employed for a decade as Episcopal priests in large urban parishes, chiefly engaged in pastoral care, education, and spiritual direction.

Prior to attending theological school, Tom spent many years as a teacher of interpersonal communications and later opened a counseling practice. Mary was co-owner of a vocational rehabilitation business, and co-founder and director of the first shelter for battered women in Maine.

For the past sixteen years, the Cushmans have worked as private practice counselors in Portland, Maine, living on nearby Chebeague Island.

SUGGESTED READING

Brené Brown, *Daring Greatly: How the Courage to Be Vulnerable Transforms the Way We Live, Love, Parent and Lead*, Gotham Books, New York, 2012.

James Hollis, *Finding Meaning in the Second Half of Life*, Gotham Books, New York, 2005.

James Hollis, *What Matters Most: Living a More Considered Life*, Gotham Books, New York, 2009.

Susan Jeffers, *Feel the Fear and Do It Anyway*, Ballantine Books, New York, 2007.

Ernest Kurtz and Katherine Ketcham, *The Spirituality of Imperfection: Storytelling and the Search for Meaning*, Bantam, New York, 2002.

Harriet Lerner, *The Dance of Intimacy*, Harper & Row, New York, 1989.

Harriet Lerner, *Marriage Rules: A Manual for the Married and the Coupled Up*, Gotham Books, New York, 2012.

Rollo May, *Love and Will*, W.W. Norton, New York, 2007.

Hal Runkel, *Scream-Free Marriage: Calming Down, Growing Up, and Getting Closer*, Crown, New York, 2011.

John A. Sanford, *The Invisible Partners: How the Male and Female in Each of Us Affects our Relationships*, Paulist Press, New York, 1980.

Maggie Scarf, *Intimate Partners: Patterns in Love and Marriage*, Ballantine Books, New York, 1988.

Susan Scott, *Fierce Conversations: Achieving Success at Work and in Life, One Conversation at a Time*, Berkley Books, New York, 2004.

Made in the USA
Middletown, DE
22 January 2020